The Beatles
J-Y

T0088602

ISBN 978-1-4234-9467-6

7777 W. BLUEMOUND RD. P.O. BOX 13819 MILWAUKEE, WI 53213

Visit Hal Leonard Online at
www.halleonard.com

Contents

How to Use This Book

Piano Chord Songbooks include the lyrics and chords for each song. The melody of the first phrase of each song is also shown.

First, play the melody excerpt to get you started in the correct key. Then, sing the song, playing the chords that are shown above the lyrics.

Chords can be voiced in many different ways. For any chords that are unfamiliar, refer to the diagram that is provided for each chord. It shows the notes that you should play with your right hand. With your left hand, simply play the note that matches the name of the chord. For example, to play a C chord, play C-E-G in your right hand, and play a C in your left hand.

You will notice that some chords are *slash chords*; for example, C/G. With your right hand, play the chord that matches the note on the left side of the slash. With your left hand, play the note on the right side of the slash. So, to play a C/G chord, play a C chord (C-E-G) in your right hand, and play a G in your left hand.

Let It Be

Words and Music by John Lennon
and Paul McCartney

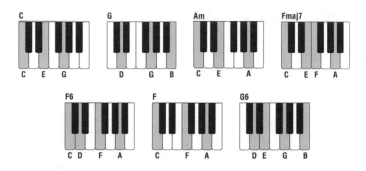

Verse 1

      C   **G**
When I find myself in times of trouble

Am   **Fmaj7**   **F6**
Mother Mary comes to me

C   **G**
Speaking words of wis - dom,

       F   **C**
Let it be.

                    G
And in my hour of dark - ness

       Am   **Fmaj7**   **F6**
She is standing right in front of me

C   **G**
Speaking words of wisdom,

       F   **C**
Let it be.

Chorus 1

          Am   **G6**
Let it be,___ let it be,

          Fmaj7   **C**
Ah, let it be,___ let it be.

             G
Whisper words of wisdom,

      F **C**
Let it be.

Verse 2

        C   **G**
And when the broken heart - ed people

Am   **Fmaj7**   **F6**
Living in the world___ agree,

C   **G**
There will be an an - swer,

      F **C**
Let it be.

                   G
For though they may be part-ed there is

Am   **Fmaj7**   **F6**
Still a chance that they___ will see

C   **G**
There will be an an-swer,

      F **C**
Let it be.

Chorus 2

          Am   **G6**
Let it be,___ let it be,

          Fmaj7   **C**
Ah, let it be,___ let it be.

                G
Yeah, there will be an an - swer,

      F **C**
Let it be.

           C   **G**

Verse 3   And when the night is cloud - y

               Am   **Fmaj7**   **F6**

There is still a light that shines on me;

C   **G**

Shine until tomor - row,

       F **C**

Let it be.

                  G

I wake up to the sound__ of music;

Am   **Fmaj7**   **F6**

Mother Mary comes__ to me,

C   **G**

Speaking words of wisdom,

       F **C**

Let it be.

             Am   **G6**

Chorus 3   Let it be,__ let it be,

               Fmaj7   **C**

Ah, let it be,__ let it be.

                     G

Yeah, there will be an an - swer,

       F **C**

Let it be.

             Am   **G6**

Let it be,__ let it be,

               Fmaj7   **C**

Ah, let it be,__ let it be.

                  G

Whisper words of wisdom,

       F **C** **F** **C** **G** **F** **C**

Let it be.

Julia

Words and Music by John Lennon
and Paul McCartney

Half of what I say is mean-ing - less,

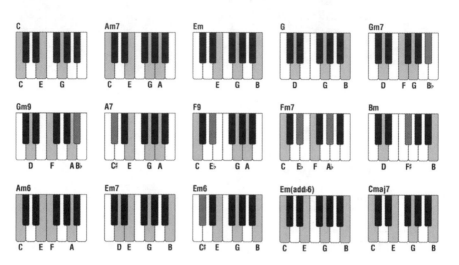

Chorus 1

C   Am7   Em
Half of what I say is meaning-less,

C   Am7   Em G C
But I say it just to reach you, Ju - lia.

Verse 1

C   Am7 Gm7 Gm9 A7   F9   Fm7
Ju - lia, Ju - lia, ocean child, calls me.

C   Am7   Em G C
So I sing a song of love, Ju - lia.

Verse 2

C   Am7 Gm7   Gm9 A7   F9   Fm7
Ju - lia,   sea-shell eyes, windy smile, calls me.

C   Am7   Em G C
So I sing a song of love, Ju - lia.

Bridge

Bm   C
Her hair of floating sky is shimmering,

Am7   Am6
Glimmering

Em7 Em6 Em(add♭6) Em
In the sun.

Verse 3

C   Am7 Gm7   Gm9 A7   F9   Fm7
Ju - lia, Ju - lia,   morning moon, touch me.

C   Am7   Em G C
So I sing a song of love, Ju   -   lia.

Chorus 2

C   Am7   Em
When I cannot sing my heart,

C   Am7   Em G C
I can only speak my mind, Ju   -   lia.

Verse 4

C   Am7 Gm7   Gm9 A7   F9   Fm7
Ju - lia,   sleeping sand, silent cloud, touch me.

C   Am7   Em G C
So I sing a song of love, Ju   -   lia.

Outro

Gm7   Gm9   A7
Mm,

F9   Fm7
Calls me.

C   Am7
So I sing a song of love

   Em   C
For Ju - lia.

Em   C
Ju - lia.

Em G Cmaj7
Ju - lia.

Lady Madonna

Words and Music by John Lennon
and Paul McCartney

Melody:

La - dy   Ma-don -   na,

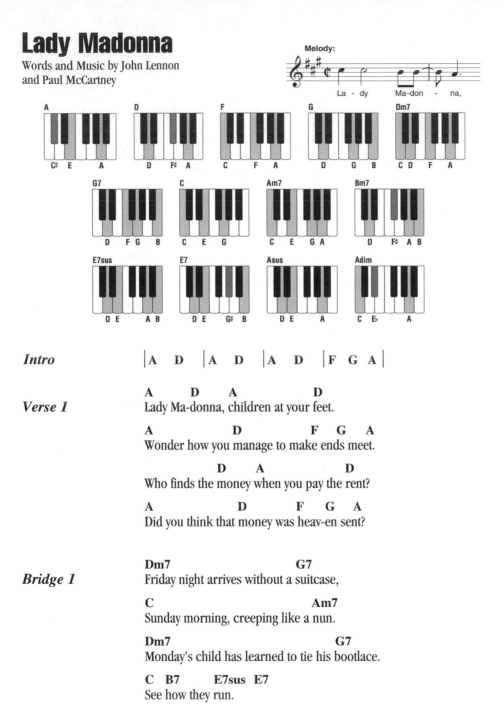

Intro

| A   D | A   D | A   D | F   G   A |

Verse 1

   A   D   A   D
Lady Ma-donna, children at your feet.

   A   D   F G A
Wonder how you manage to make ends meet.

                D   A   D
Who finds the money when you pay the rent?

   A   D   F   G   A
Did you think that money was heav-en sent?

Bridge 1

Dm7   G7
Friday night arrives without a suitcase,

C   Am7
Sunday morning, creeping like a nun.

Dm7   G7
Monday's child has learned to tie his bootlace.

C B7   E7sus E7
See how they run.

Verse 2

```
A       D     A          D
Lady Ma-donna, baby at your breast.

A                D          F G  A
Wonder how you manage to feed the rest.

|A   D  |A   D  |A   D   |F  G  A |
```

Solo

```
|Dm7  |G7   |C    |Am7  |Dm7  |G7     |
```

```
C  B7      E7sus  E7
See how they run.
```

Verse 3

```
A       D     A          D
Lady Ma-donna, lying on the bed.

A           D          F G   A
Listen to the music playing in your head.

|A   D  |A   D  |A   D   |F  G  A |
```

Bridge 2

```
Dm7                       G7
Tuesday afternoon is never-ending.

C                           Am7
Wednesday morning, papers didn't come.

Dm7                         G7
Thursday night, your stockings needed mending.

C  B7      E7sus  E7
See how they run.
```

Verse 4

```
A       D     A             D
Lady Ma-donna, children at your feet.

A                D          F  G   A  Asus  Adim  A
Wonder how you manage to make ends meet.
```

Outro

```
|A   Asus  |Ao Asus   A
```

Like Dreamers Do

Words and Music by John Lennon
and Paul McCartney

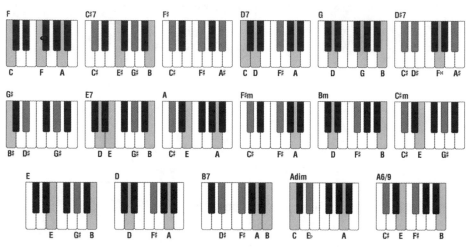

Intro

| F   C#7 F#   D7 | G   D#7 G#   E7 |

Verse 1

    A   F#m
I, I saw a girl in my dreams,

        Bm   C#m E
And so   it seems that I will love   her.

     A   F#m
Oh you, you are that girl in my dreams,

        Bm   C#m E
And so   it seems that I will love   you.

Chorus 1

        A   C#7
And I waited for your kiss,

        Bm   E7
Waited for the bliss

    N.C.   A
Like dreamers do.

PIANO CHORD SONGBOOK

Bridge 1	**D E**
	And I,
	
	  A
	I, I, I, I,
	
	    Bm B7
	Oh, I'll be there, yeah.
	
	   E7
	Waiting for you, you, you, you, you, you.

Verse 2	**A** **F♯m**
	You, you came just one dream ago,
	
	   Bm **C♯m E**
	And now I know that I will love you.
	
	  A **F♯m**
	Oh, I knew when you first said hello,
	
	   Bm **C♯m E**
	That's how I know that I will love you.

Chorus 2	*Repeat Chorus 1*
Bridge 2	*Repeat Bridge 1*
Verse 3	*Repeat Verse 2*

Chorus 3	**A** **C♯7**
	And I waited for your kiss,
	
	    Bm **E7**
	Waited for the bliss
	
	N.C. **A**
	Like dreamers do.
	
	Adim **A**
	  Oh, like dreamers do,
	
	Adim **A**
	  Like dreamers do.

Outro	|A○ |F C♯7 F♯ D7 |G D♯7 G♯ E7 |A |A6/9

Little Child

Words and Music by John Lennon
and Paul McCartney

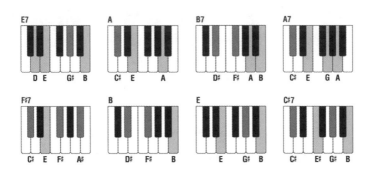

Intro | E7 | A | E7 | | |

Verse 1
       E7
Little child, little child,

                 A   **E7**
Little child, won't you dance with me?

B7   **A7**
I'm so sad and lonely.

F#7   **B**
Baby, take a chance with me.

Verse 2
       E7
Little child, little child,

                 A   **E7**
Little child, won't you dance with me?

B7   **A7**
I'm so sad and lonely.

F#7   **B7**   **E**
Baby, take a chance with me.

Bridge 1

        E   B7
If you want someone to make you feel so fine,

            E7
Then we'll have some fun when you're mine, all mine.

          F#7   B
So come on, come on, come on!

Verse 3   *Repeat Verse 2*

Solo

E7				A7		
E7		B7	A7	F#7	B7	

Bridge 2

           E   B7
When you're by my side, you're the only one.

            E7
Don't you run and hide, just come on, come on.

          F#7   B
Yeah, come on, come on, come on.

Verse 4

            E7
Little child, little child,

                          A   E7
Little child, won't you dance with me?

B7   A7
I'm so sad and lonely.

F#7   B7   E   C#7
Baby, take a chance with me, oh yeah.

F#7   B7   E   C#7
Baby, take a chance with me, oh yeah.

F#7   B7   E   C#7
Baby, take a chance with me, oh yeah. *Fade out*

The Long and Winding Road

Words and Music by John Lennon
and Paul McCartney

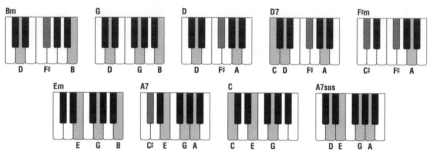

Verse 1

      Bm   **G/A**
The long and winding road

      D   **D7**   **G**
That leads to your door

     F#m   **Bm**
Will never disap-pear.

Em   **A7**   **C/D**
  I've seen that road be-fore.

G **F#m**   **Bm**
  It always leads me here,

Em   **A7** **A7sus** **D**
  Lead me to   your door.

Verse 2

      Bm   **G/A**
The wild and windy night

        D D7   **G**
That the rain washed a-way,

     F#m Bm
Has left a pool of tears

Em   **A7**   **C/D**
  Crying for the day.

G   **F#m**   **Bm**
  Why leave me standing here?

Em   **A7**   **A7sus D**
Let me know the   way.

Bridge 1

D/A   G
Many times I've been alone,

    D/F♯   Em   A7
And many times I've cried.

D/A   G
Anyway, you'll never know

    D/F♯   Em   A7
The many ways I've tried.

Verse 3

       Bm   G/A
And still they lead me back

      D D7   G
To the long, winding road.

  F♯m   Bm
You left me standing here

Em   A7   C/D
A long, long time ago.

G   F♯m   Bm
Don't leave me wait-ing here,

Em   A7 A7sus D
Lead me to your   door.

Bridge 2

‖: D/A G | D/F♯ Em A7 :‖

Verse 4

      Bm   G/A
But still they lead me back

      D D7   G
To the long, winding road.

  F♯m   Bm
You left me standing here

Em   A7   C/D
A long, long time ago.

G   F♯m   Bm
Don't keep me wait-ing here,

Em   A7   D
Lead me to your door.

G/A   D
(Yeah, yeah, yeah, yeah.)

Long Long Long

Words and Music by
George Harrison

Melody:

It's been a long, — long,

Em   G   D   A

E G B   D G B   D F♯ A   C♯ E A

F♯m   A7   Asus

C♯ F♯ A   C♯ E G A   D E A

Intro |Em G |Em D |A |

                     G   F♯m Em D Em/G D

Verse 1   It's been a long, long,   long time.

                 A   Em   D A
                 How could I ever have lost you,

                 Em   D   A
                 When I   loved you?

                     G   F♯m Em D   Em/G D
                 It took a long, long, long time.

                 A   Em   D A
                 Now I'm so happy I found you,

                 Em   D   A   A7
                 How I love you.

                 G   D   A   Em

Bridge   So many tears I was searching,

                 G   D   A   Em G A
                 So many tears I was wast-ing. Oh, oh!

                     G   F♯m Em D   Em/G D

Verse 2   Now I can see you,   be you.

                 A   Em   D A
                 How can I ever mis-place you?

                 Em   D   A   Em   D   A
                 How I want you,   how I love you.

                 Em   D   A
                 You know that I need you.

                 Em   D   A   Asus
                 Oh, I love you.   Ah.

Lucy in the Sky with Diamonds

Words and Music by John Lennon
and Paul McCartney

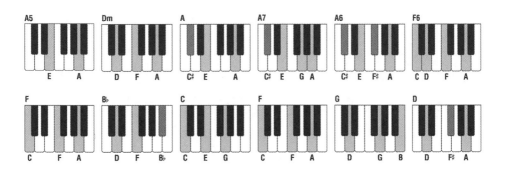

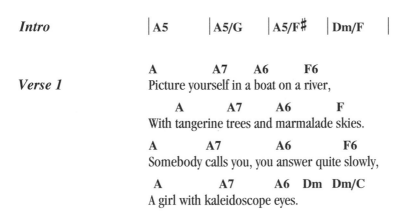

Intro |A5 |A5/G |A5/F# |Dm/F |

         A   A7 A6   F6

Verse 1   Picture yourself in a boat on a river,

           A   A7 A6   F

         With tangerine trees and marmalade skies.

         A   A7   A6   F6

         Somebody calls you, you answer quite slowly,

          A   A7   A6 Dm Dm/C

         A girl with kaleidoscope eyes.

	Bb	C
Pre-Chorus 1	Cellophane flowers of yellow and green,	

Pre-Chorus 1

Bb   C
Cellophane flowers of yellow and green,

F   Bb
Towering over your head.

C   G
Look for the girl with the sun in her eyes,

           D
And she's gone.

Chorus 1

G   C   D
Lucy in the sky with diamonds.

G   C   D
Lucy in the sky with diamonds.

G   C   D
Lucy in the sky with diamonds.

D A
Ah, ah.

Verse 2

A   A7   A6   F6
Follow her down to a bridge by a fountain,

      A   A7   A6   F
Where rocking horse people eat marshmallow pies.

A   A7   A6   F6
Everyone smiles as you drift past the flowers,

     A   A7   A6 Dm Dm/C
That grow so in-credibly high.

Pre-Chorus 2

Bb   C
Newspaper taxis ap-pear on the shore,

F   Bb
Waiting to take you a-way.

C   G
Climb in the back with your head in the clouds,

           D
And you're gone.

Chorus 2   *Repeat Chorus 1*

Verse 3

A   A7   A6   F6
Picture your-self on a train in a station,

   A   A7   A6   F
With plasticine porters with looking glass ties.

A   A7   A6   F6
Suddenly someone is there at the turnstile,

   A   A7   A6 Dm
The girl with ka-leidoscope eyes.

Chorus 3

  G   C   D
‖: Lucy in the sky with diamonds.

G   C   D
Lucy in the sky with diamonds.

G   C   D
Lucy in the sky with diamonds.

D A
Ah, ah. :‖ *Repeat and fade*

Long Tall Sally

Words and Music by Enotris Johnson,
Richard Penniman and Robert Blackwell

Gon-na   tell Aunt Mar - y   'bout Un -cle John.

Verse 1

       G5 N.C.   **G5 N.C.**
Gonna tell Aunt Mary 'bout Uncle John.

G5 N.C.
Said he had the mis'ry, but he got a lot of fun.

    C7
Oh, ba - by,

       G7
Yeah now, ba - by.

      D7   **C7**   **G7**
Woo, ba - by,   some fun tonight.

Verse 2

      G5 N.C.   **G5 N.C.**
Well, I saw Uncle John with blond headed Sally.

   G5 N.C.
He saw Aunt Mary comin' and he ducked back in the alley.

    C7
Oh, ba - by,

       G7
Yeah now, ba - by.

    D7
Woo, ba - by,

C7   **G7**
   Have some fun tonight. ___ Ah!

Solo 1

G7				
C7		G7		
D7	C7	G7		

Verse 3

      G5 N.C.   **G5 N.C.**
Well, Long Tall Sally's built a,   a pretty sweet.

      G5 N.C.
She's got   ev'rything that Uncle John needs.

  C7
Oh, baby,

      G7
Yeah now, ba - by.

   D7
Woo, ba - by,

C7   **G7**
  Some fun tonight. __ Ah!

Solo 2   *Repeat Solo 1*

      G7
Outro   Well, we're gonna have some fun tonight.

We're gonna have some fun tonight.

  C7
Oo, __ ev'rything's all right.

     G7
Yeah, we'll have some fun tonight.

D7   **C7**   **G7**
Have some fun,   yeah.

Well, we're gonna have some fun tonight.

I said, we'll have some fun tonight.

  C7
Oo, __ ev'rything's all right.

     G7
Yeah, we'll have some fun tonight.

     D7   **C7**   **G7**   **G9**
Yeah, we'll have some fun, __ some fun tonight.

Love Me Do

Words and Music by John Lennon
and Paul McCartney

Melody:

Love,   love   me   do. ___

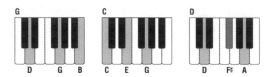

Intro

| G | C | G | C | G | C | G | | |

Chorus 1

G   C
Love, love me do.

       G   C
You know I love you.

       G   C
I'll always be true.

So please,

N.C.   G   C   G   C
Love me do. ___ Oh, love me do.

Chorus 2   *Repeat Chorus 1*

Bridge

D
Someone to love,

C   G
Somebody new.

D
Someone to love,

C   G
Someone like you.

	G C

Chorus 3

             G   C
Love, love me do.

                G   C
You know I love you.

             G   C
I'll always be true.

So please,

N.C.   **G**   **C**   **G**
Love me do. ____ Oh, love me do.

Solo

‖: **D** | | | **C** | **G**   :‖

| | | | **D** |

Chorus 4

             G   C
Love, love me do.

                G   C
You know I love you.

             G   C
I'll always be true.

So please,

N.C.   **G**   **C**   **G**   **C**
Love me do. ____ Oh, love me do.

                G   C
‖: Yeah, love me do.

             G   C
Oh, love me do. :‖   *Repeat and fade*

Love You To

Words and Music by
George Harrison

Melody:

Each _ day ___ just   goes _   so   fast. ___

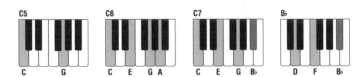

C5   C6   C7   Bb
C   G   C   E   G   A   C   E   G   Bb   D   F   Bb

Intro   ‖: C5 | | | :‖

Verse 1
C6   C5
Each day just goes so fast.

C6   C5
I turn around, it's past.

C6   C5   C7   C6   C7 C5
You don't get time to hang a sign on me.

Chorus 1
Bb   C5   Bb   C5
Love me while you can,

Bb   C5   Bb   C5
Before I'm a dead old man.

Verse 2
C6   C5
A lifetime is so short.

C6   C5
A new one can't be bought.

C6   C5   C7   C6   C7 C5
But what you've got means such a lot to me.

	Bb C5 Bb C5
Chorus 2	Make love all day long.

           Bb   C5   Bb   C5
Make love singing songs.

Interlude   ‖: C5 | | | | :‖

Chorus 3   *Repeat Chorus 2*

           C6   C5
Verse 3   There's people stand-ing 'round,

           C6   C5
Who'll screw you in the ground.

           C6   C5   C7   C6
They'll fill you in with all their sins,

           C7   C5
You'll see.

           Bb   C5   Bb   C5
Chorus 4   I'll make love to you.

           Bb   C5   Bb   C5
If you want me to.

Outro   ‖: C5 | | | :‖ *Repeat and fade*

Lovely Rita

Words and Music by John Lennon
and Paul McCartney

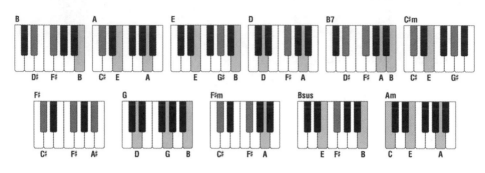

Intro

|B |A |E |B |

Ah.

B   A
Lovely Rita meter maid.

E   B
Lovely Rita meter maid.

Chorus 1

E   D   A
Lovely Rita meter maid,

E   B7
Nothing can stand be-tween us.

C#m   F#   B7
When it gets dark, I tow your heart a-way.

Verse 1

E   A
 Standing by a parking meter,

D   G
 When I caught a glimpse of Rita

E   B7
Filling in a ticket in her little white book.

Verse 2

E   A
 In a cap, she looked much older.

D   G
 And the bag a-cross her shoulder

E   B7   E C#m F#m B
Made her look a little like a military man.

Chorus 2

E   D   A
Lovely Rita meter maid,

E   B7
May I enquire dis-creetly,

C#m   F#   B7
When are you free to take some tea with me?

Bsus B
Ah.

Solo

|E   D A |E B7 |C#m F# |B   B7 |
Rita!

Verse 3

E   A
Took her out and tried to win her.

D   G
  Had a laugh, and over dinner

E   B7
Told her I would really like to see her again.

Verse 4

E   A
Got the bill and Rita paid it.

D   G
  Took her home, I nearly made it.

E   B7   E C#m F#m B
Sitting on a sofa with a sister or two.   Oh.

Chorus 3

E   D   A
Lovely Rita meter maid,

E   B7
Where would I be with-out you?

C#m   F#   (B)
Give us a wink and make me think of you.

Outro

B   A
||: Lovely Rita meter maid.

E   B
Lovely Rita meter maid. :||

||: Am | | | :||

| | |A

Magical Mystery Tour

Words and Music by John Lennon
and Paul McCartney

Roll up, _____

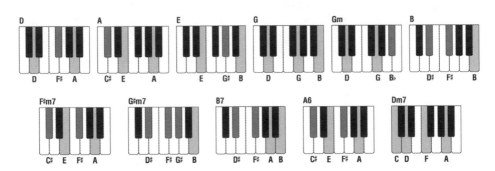

Intro |D |A |

E
(Roll up, roll up for the Magical Mystery Tour.

Step right this way!)

Verse 1

    E   G   A
Roll up, _____ roll up for the Mystery Tour.

    E   G   A
Roll up, _____ roll up for the Mystery Tour.

    E
Roll up, _____ (And that's and invitation.)

    G   A
Roll up, _____ for the Mystery Tour.

    E
Roll up, _____ (To make a reservation.)

    G   A
Roll up, _____ for the Mystery Tour.

Bridge 1

D   **D/C**
The Magical Mystery Tour

G/B   **Gm/B♭**
Is waiting to take you a-way,

D/A   **A**
Waiting to take you a-way.

Verse 2

E   **G**   **A**
Roll up, _____ roll up for the Mystery Tour.

E   **G**   **A**
Roll up, _____ roll up for the Mystery Tour.

E
Roll up, _____ (We've got everything you need.)

G   **A**
Roll up, _____ for the Mystery Tour.

E
Roll up, _____ (Satisfaction guaranteed.)

G   **A**
Roll up, _____ for the Mystery Tour.

Bridge 2

D   **D/C**
The Magical Mystery Tour

G/B   **Gm/B♭**
Is hoping to take you a-way,

D/A   **A**
Hoping to take you a-way.

Interlude

B			F#m7		

(Mystery   trip.)

B		F#m7		G#m7	A		B7	

Verse 3	**E** **G** **A** Ah, _____ the Magical Mystery Tour.

E   **G**   **A**
Roll up, _____ roll up for the Mystery Tour.

E
Roll up, _____ (And that's an invitation.)

G   **A**
Roll up, _____ for the Mystery Tour.

E
Roll up, _____ (To make a reservation.)

G   **A**
Roll up, _____ for the Mystery Tour.

Bridge 3	**D** **D/C** The Magical Mystery Tour

  G/B   **Gm/B♭**
Is coming to take you a-way,

D/A   **A6**
Coming to take you a-way.

D   **D/C**
The Magical Mystery Tour

  G/B   **Gm/B♭**
Is dying to take you a-way,

D/A   **A6**
Dying to take you a-way,

          D
Take you to-day.

Outro	‖: **Dm7** | | | :‖ *Repeat and fade*

Martha My Dear

Words and Music by John Lennon
and Paul McCartney

Mar - tha, ___ my dear, though I spend ___ my days in...

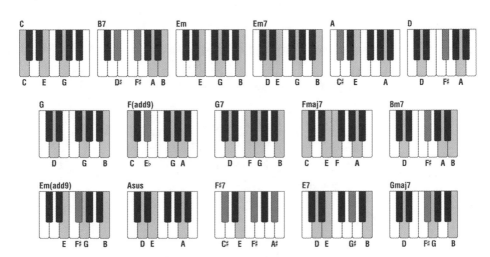

Intro

| C | | B7 | Em Em7 A | D | |
| G F(add9) | G7 Fmaj7 | G7 Fmaj7 | G G7 | |

Verse 1

C
Martha, my dear,

          B7   Em   Em7   A
Though I spend my days in conver-sation,

D   G
Please remember me.

F(add9)   G7
Martha, my love,

Fmaj7   G7
Don't forget me,

Fmaj7   G7
Martha, my dear.

Verse 2

Bm7   Em(add9)
Hold your head up, you silly girl,

D
Look what you've done.

     Asus   A
When you find yourself in the thick of it,

Asus   A   F#7 Bm7
Help yourself to a bit of what is all   around you,

   Em(add9)
Silly girl.

Verse 3

   Bm7   E7
Take a good look a-round you,

   Bm7   E7
Take a good look, you're bound to see

   Gmaj7/A
That you and me

   Gmaj7   Bm7
Were meant to be for each oth-er,

   Em(add9)   C
Silly girl.

Interlude

C		B7	Em Em7 A	D	

G F(add9)	G7 Fmaj7	G7 Fmaj7	G G7

Verse 4

Bm7   Em(add9)
Hold your hand out, you silly girl,

D
See what you've done.

            Asus   A
When you find yourself in the thick of it,

Asus   A   F#7 Bm7
Help yourself to a bit of what is all   around you,

     Em(add9)   C G7 C
Silly girl.

Verse 5

C
Martha, my dear,

             B7   Em   Em7 A
You have always been my inspir-ation,

D   G
Please be good to me.

F(add9)   G7
Martha, my love,

Fmaj7   G7
Don't forget me,

Fmaj7   G7
Martha, my dear.

Outro | C C/B C/A C/G | C

Matchbox

Words and Music by
Carl Lee Perkins

Intro |A | | | |

Verse 1
    A
I'm sittin' here watchin',

Matchbox hole in my clothes.

    D
Oh, __ sittin' watchin',

                 A
Matchbox hole in my __ clothes.

  E7
I ain't got no matches;

D   **A**
Sure got a long way to go.

Verse 2
            A
Well, I'm an old __ poor boy and

I ain't got a home.

       D
I'm an old __ poor boy and I'm a

           A
Long way from home.

  E7
And ev'rything I do

    D   **A**
Turns __ out mighty wrong. *All right, John.*

Solo 1   *Repeat Verse 1 (Instrumental)*

Solo 2   *Repeat Verse 1 (Instrumental)*

                                       A

Verse 3   Well, if you don't want my peaches, honey,

                       Please don't shake my tree.

                     D

If you don't wanna drink those peaches, honey,

                                   A

Please don't mess around my __ tree.

                  E7

I got news __ for you, baby.

                D   **A**

Leave __ you here in misery.

                                     A

Verse 4   Well, I said I'm sittin' here watchin',

                       Matchbox hole in my clothes.

                     D

Oh, __ sittin' watchin',

                                  A

Matchbox hole in my __ clothes.

                 E7

I ain't got no matches;

D   **A**   **A6**

Sure got a long way to go.

Maxwell's Silver Hammer

Words and Music by John Lennon
and Paul McCartney

Melody:

Joan was quiz-zi-cal, stud-ied pat-a-phys-i-cal...

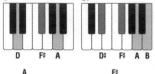   

D · B7 · Em · Em7 · A7 · E7

A · F# · Bm · D7 · G

Verse 1

  D   **D/C#**
Joan was quizzical,

B7   **Em**   **Em7**
Studied pataphysical science in the home.

A7
Late nights all alone with a test-tube,

D   **A7**
Oh, oh, oh, oh.

D   **D/C#** **B7**
Maxwell Edison, majoring in medicine,

Em   **Em7**
Calls her on the phone.

A7   **D**   **A7**
"Can I take you out to the pictures, Jo-o-o-an?"

    E7
But as she's getting ready to go,

   A7
A knock comes on the door.

Chorus 1

  D
Bang, bang, Maxwell's silver hammer

    E7
Came down upon her head.

A7
Clang, clang, Maxwell's silver hammer

     Em   **A7**   **D** **A** **D**
Made sure that she was dead.

Interlude |D F#/C# |Bm D7/A |G |D |

Verse 2

D   D/C#   B7
Back in school again, Maxwell plays the fool again,

Em   Em7
Teacher gets annoyed.

A7   D   A7
Wishing to avoid an unpleasant sce-e-e-ene.

D   D/C#   B7
She tells Max to stay when the class has gone away,

Em   Em7
So he waits behind.

A7   D   A7
Writing fifty times, I must not be so-o-o-o.

    E7
But when she turns her back on the boy,

    A7
He creeps up from behind.

Chorus 2

D
Bang, bang, Maxwell's silver hammer

    E7
Came down upon her head.

A7
Clang, clang, Maxwell's silver hammer

        Em   A7
Made sure that she was dead.

Solo |D | |E7 | |
           |A7 | |Em7 A7 |D |
           |D F#/C# |Bm D7/A |G |D |

Verse 3

D D/C#   B7
P.C. Thirty-One said,

"We've caught a dirty one."
Em   Em7
Maxwell stands alone.

A7
Painting testimonial pictures,

D   A7
Oh, oh, oh, oh.

D   D/C# B7
Rose and Valerie, screaming from the gallery,

Em   Em7
Say he must go free.

  A7   D   A7
The judge does not agree, and he tells them so-o-o-o.

        E7
But as the words are leaving his lips,

  A7
A noise comes from behind.

Chorus 3

D
Bang, bang, Maxwell's silver hammer

      E7
Came down upon his head.

A7
Clang, clang, Maxwell's silver hammer

    Em   A7
Made sure that he was dead.

Outro

        D
Wo-wo-wo-woh.

|D |E7 | |A7 | |Em7 A7|D A D|

    F#/C# Bm D7/A G D A D
Sil - ver   ham - mer   man.

Michelle

Words and Music by John Lennon
and Paul McCartney

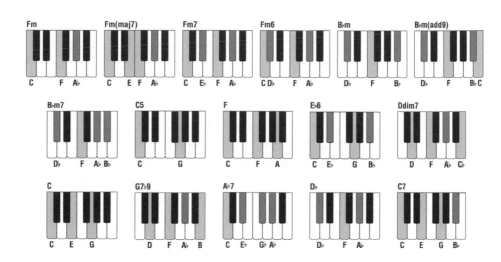

Intro | Fm Fm(maj7) | Fm7 Fm6 | B♭m B♭m(add9) B♭m B♭m7 | C5 |

                F   **B♭m7**

Verse 1   Michelle, ma belle.

                E♭6   **Ddim7**   **C**
                These are words that go together well,

                G7♭9 **C**
                My Mi-chelle.

                F   **B♭m7**

Verse 2   Michelle, ma belle.

                E♭6   **Ddim7**   **C**
                Sont les mots qui vont très bien en-semble,

                G7♭9   **C**
                Très bien en-semble.

Bridge 1

Fm
I love you, I love you, I love you.

A♭7   D♭
  That's all I want to say.

C7   Fm
  Until I find a way,

      Fm   Fm(maj7) Fm7   Fm6
I will say the only   words I know

      B♭m B♭m(add9) B♭m B♭m7 C5
That you'll   un - der - stand.

Verse 3

Repeat Verse 2

Bridge 2

Fm
I need to, I need to, I need to,

A♭7   D♭
  I need to make you see,

C7   Fm
  Oh, what you mean to me.

      Fm Fm(maj7) Fm7   Fm6
Un-til I do I'm   hoping you

      B♭m B♭m(add9) B♭m B♭m7 C5
Will know   what I   mean.

Solo

Fm   B♭m7
  I love you.

| E♭6 | Ddim7 | C G7♭9 | C |

Bridge 3

Fm
I want you, I want you, I want you.

A♭7   D♭
 I think you know by now,

C7   Fm
 I'll get to you some-how.

   Fm Fm(maj7) Fm7   Fm6
Un-til I do   I'm   telling you,

   B♭m B♭m(add9) B♭m B♭m7 C5
So you'll   un - der - stand.

Verse 4

F   B♭m7
Michelle,   ma belle.

E♭6   Ddim7   C
Sont les mots qui vont très bien en-semble,

G7♭9   C
Très bien en-semble.

      Fm   Fm(maj7) Fm7   Fm6
And I will say the only   words I know

   B♭m B♭m(add9) B♭m B♭m7 C5
That you'll   un - der - stand.

    F
My Mi-chelle.

Outro

| B♭m7 | E♭6 | Ddim7 | C   G7♭9 |
| B♭Fm7 | E♭6 | *Fade out* | |

Mean Mr. Mustard

Words and Music by John Lennon
and Paul McCartney

Melody:

Mean Mis - ter Mus-tard sleeps   in   the park,

E7   B7   C7   C#7   D7

D E   G♯ B   D♯ F♯ A B   C   E   G   B♭   C♯   E♯ G♯ B   C D   F♯   A

Verse 1

E7
Mean Mr. Mustard sleeps in the park,

Shaves in the dark

Trying to save paper.

B7   **C7   C♯7**
Sleeps in a hole in the road.

D7   **C7   C♯7**
  Saving up to buy some clothes.

B7
  Keeps a ten bob note up his nose.

    E7   **C7   B7**
Such a mean old man.

    E7   **C7   B7**
Such a mean old man.

E7

Verse 2 His sister Pam works in a shop.

She never stops,

She's a go-getter.

B7   **C7 C#7**
Takes him out to look at the Queen.

D7   **C7 C#7**
  Only place that he's ever been.

B7
  Always shouts out something obscene.

     E7   **C7** **B7**
Such a dirty old man.

E7   **C7** **B7**
Dirty old man.

Misery

Words and Music by John Lennon
and Paul McCartney

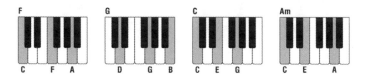

Intro

F   G
The world is treating me bad,

C   Am G
Misery.

Verse 1

C   F
I'm the kind of guy

     C   F
Who never used to cry.

                  G
The world is treating me bad.

C   Am
Misery.

Verse 2

     C   F
I've lost her now for sure,

 C   F
I won't see her no more.

          G
It's gonna be a drag.

C
Misery.

Bridge 1

Am   C
I'll remember all the little things we've done.

Am   G
Can't she see she'll always be the only one,

Only one?

Verse 3

C   F
Send her back to me.

         C   F
'Cause everyone can see,

                 G
Without her I will be

  C
In misery.

Bridge 2

Am   C
I'll remember all the little things we've done.

Am   G
She'll remember and she'll miss her only one,

Lonely one.

Verse 4

C   F
Send her back to me.

         C   F
'Cause everyone can see,

                 G
Without her I will be

  C
In misery,

Am   C   Am
Oh, in misery. Ooh,

   C
My misery.

Am   C
La, la, la, la, la, la, misery.

Mr. Moonlight

Words and Music by
Roy Lee Johnson

Melody:

Mis - ter _____ Moon - light.

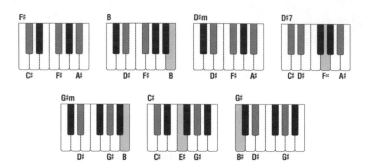

Intro

N.C.
Mr. Moonlight.

| F# | | |

Verse 1

F#
You came to me one summer night,

B   **F#**
And from your beam you made my dream.

D#m
And from the world you sent my girl,

B   **F#** **N.C.**
And from above you sent us love.

B
And now she is mine;

F#   **D#7**
I think you're fine,

        G#m
Because we love you,

C# **N.C.**   **F#**
    Mister Moon-light.

Bridge 1

   F#
Mister Moonlight, come again please.

                 N.C.
Here I am on my knees, begging if you please.

Verse 2

   B
 And the night you don't come my way,

  F#   **D#7**
I __ pray and pray more each day,

    G#m
Because we love you,

 C# **N.C.**   **F#**
 Mister Moon-light.

Solo

F#				
			N.C.	

Verse 3   *Repeat Verse 2*

Bridge 2   *Repeat Bridge 1*

Verse 4   *Repeat Verse 2*

          F#
Outro   ‖: Mister Moonlight. :‖ *Repeat and fade*

Money
(That's What I Want)

Words and Music by Berry Gordy
and Janie Bradford

Melody:

The best _ things in   life are   free. _

E7   B7   A7   E   A

Intro |E7 | | | |
               |B7 |A7 |E7 |B7 |

                    E   A   E
Verse 1   The best things in life are free.

                 But you can keep them for the birds and bees.

                           A7
                 Now give me mon   -   ey.
                                   (That's   what I want.)

                           E7
                 That's what I want. (That's what I want.)

                           B7   A7
                 That's what I want,   yeah.
                                   (That's what I   want.)

                 E7   B7
                    That's what I want.

	E A E
Verse 2	Your lovin' give me a thrill.

But your lovin' don't pay my bills.

       A7
Now give me mon   -   ey.
                (That's   what I want.)

       E7
That's what I want. (That's what I want.)

      B7   **A7**
That's what I want,   yeah.
            (That's what I   want.)

E7   **B7**
That's what I want.

	E A E
Verse 3	Money don't get ev'rything it's true.

What it don't get I can't use.

       A7
Now give me mon   -   ey.
                (That's   what I want.)

       E7
That's what I want. (That's what I want.)

      B7   **A7**
That's what I want,   yeah.
            (That's what I   want.)

E7   **B7**
That's what I want.

Solo	*Repeat Intro*
Verse 4	*Repeat Verse 3*

Verse 5

           E7
Well, now give me money. (That's what I want.)

                                                 A7
A lotta money.   Wow, yeah. I wanna be free.
          (That's   what I want.)

(That's what I want.)

      E7
Whole lot - ta money.
      (That's what I want.)

     B7   **A7**
That's what I want,   yeah.
          (That's what I want.)

E7   **B7**
   That's what I want.

Verse 6

           E7
Well, now give me money. (That's what I want.)

                                            A7
A lotta money.   Wow, yeah. You know I need mon - ey.
          (That's   what I want.)

                       E7
     Oh,   now give me money.
(That's what I want.)   (That's what I want.)

     B7   **A7**
That's what I want,   yeah.
          (That's what I want.)

E7
   That's what I want.

The Night Before

Words and Music by John Lennon
and Paul McCartney

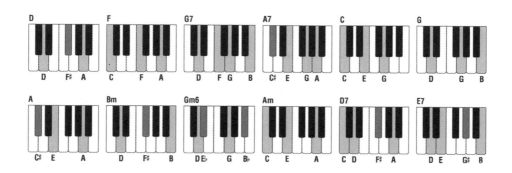

Intro | D | | F | | G7 | | A7 | | |

Verse 1

D   C
We said our good-byes,

G   A
(Ah, the night before.)

D   C
Love was in your eyes.

G   A
(Ah, the night before.)

Bm   Gm6 Bm   Gm6
Now today I find, you have changed your mind.

D   G7   D F G
Treat me like you did the night be-fore.

Verse 2

D   C
Were you telling lies?

G   A
(Ah, the night before.)

D   C
Was I so un-wise?

G   A
(Ah, the night before.)

Bm   Gm6 Bm   Gm6
When I held you near, you were so sin-cere.

D   G7   D
Treat me like you did the night be-fore.

Bridge 1

Am   D7   G   C/G G
Last night is the night I will re-member you by,

Bm   E7   A7
When I think of things we did, it makes me wanna cry.

Verse 3

D   C
We said our good-byes,

G   A
(Ah, the night before.)

D   C
Love was in your eyes.

G   A
(Ah, the night before.)

Bm   Gm6 Bm   Gm6
Now today I find, you have changed your mind.

D   G7   D F G
Treat me like you did the night be-fore,   yes…

Solo	‖: D | C | G | A :‖

Verse 4

Bm   Gm6 Bm   Gm6
When I held you near, you were so sin-cere.

D   G7   D
Treat me like you did the night be-fore.

Bridge 2   *Repeat Bridge 1*

Verse 5

D   C
Were you telling lies?

 G   A
(Ah, the night before.)

D   C
Was I so un-wise?

 G   A
(Ah, the night before.)

Bm   Gm6 Bm   Gm6
When I held you near, you were so sin-cere.

D   G7   D
Treat me like you did the night be-fore.

F   G
Like the night be-fore.

Mother Nature's Son

Words and Music by John Lennon
and Paul McCartney

Melody:

Born _ a poor _ young coun - try _ boy,

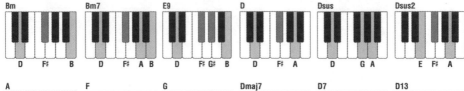

Bm   Bm7   E9   D   Dsus   Dsus2

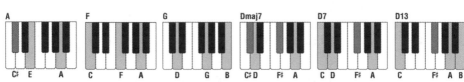

A   F   G   Dmaj7   D7   D13

Intro

Bm Bm7/A	E9/G# E9	
D Dsus	Dsus2 Dsus D	
Dsus2 D Dsus D	Dsus2 D Dsus2 D	

Verse 1

          D   Dsus   D
Born a poor young country boy,
          Bm   Bm7/A E9/G#   E9
Mother Nature's son.

          A D/A   A D/A A
All day long__ I'm sitting
                D/A   A   D/A
Sing - ing songs__ for ev - 'ryone.

| D   F/D | G/D   D | |
| F/D | G/D   D | |

Verse 2

          D   Dsus   D
Sit be-side a mountain stream,
          Bm   Bm7/A E9/G#   E9
See her waters   rise.

          A D/A   A D/A A
Lis-ten to__ the pretty
                D/A   A   D F/D G/D D
Sound__ of mu - sic as she flies.

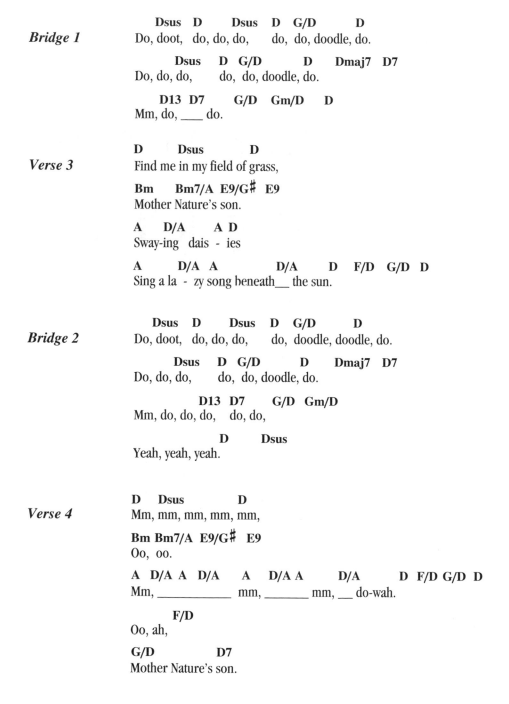

Bridge 1

Dsus D   Dsus D G/D   D
Do, doot, do, do, do,   do, do, doodle, do.

        Dsus D G/D   D   Dmaj7 D7
Do, do, do,   do, do, doodle, do.

    D13 D7   G/D Gm/D   D
Mm, do, ___ do.

Verse 3

D   Dsus   D
Find me in my field of grass,

Bm   Bm7/A E9/G♯ E9
Mother Nature's son.

A   D/A   A D
Sway-ing dais - ies

A   D/A A   D/A   D F/D G/D D
Sing a la - zy song beneath__ the sun.

Bridge 2

Dsus D   Dsus D G/D   D
Do, doot, do, do, do,   do, doodle, doodle, do.

        Dsus D G/D   D   Dmaj7 D7
Do, do, do,   do, do, doodle, do.

        D13 D7   G/D Gm/D
Mm, do, do, do, do, do,

                D   Dsus
Yeah, yeah, yeah.

Verse 4

D Dsus   D
Mm, mm, mm, mm, mm,

Bm Bm7/A E9/G♯ E9
Oo, oo.

A D/A A D/A   A   D/A A   D/A   D F/D G/D D
Mm, _____ mm, _____ mm, __ do-wah.

        F/D
Oo, ah,

G/D   D7
Mother Nature's son.

No Reply

Words and Music by John Lennon
and Paul McCartney

Melody:

This hap-pened once be - fore when I came to your door,

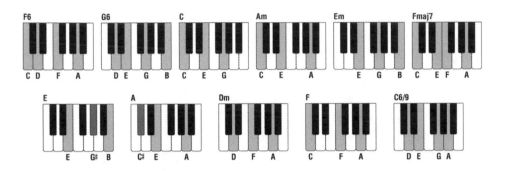

Verse 1

    N.C.   **F6**
This happened once be-fore

               G6   **C**
When I came to your door, no re-ply.

              F6
They said it wasn't you,

            G6   **C**
But I saw you peep through your window.

      Am **Em**   **Fmaj7** **Em**
I saw the light,   I saw the light.

             F6
I know that you saw me,

             G6   **C**
'Cause I looked up to see your face.

Verse 2

          F6
I tried to tele-phone.

               G6   **C**
They said you were not home, that's a lie.

               F6
'Cause I know where you've been,

       G6   **C**
I saw you walk in your door.

      Am Em   **Fmaj7 Em**
I nearly died,   I nearly died,

          F6
'Cause you walked hand in hand

       G6   **C**
With another man in my place.

Bridge

       C   **E**   **A**
If I were you, I'd realize that I

     Dm   **F**   **C**
Love you more than any other guy.

          E   **A**
And I'll forgive the lies that I

     Dm   **F**   **C**
Heard be-fore, when you gave me no re-ply.

Verse 3

          F6
I tried to tele-phone.

               G6   **C**
They said you were not home, that's a lie.

               F6
'Cause I know where you've been,

       G6   **C**
And I saw you walk in your door.

      Am Em   **Fmaj7 Em**
I nearly died,   I nearly died,

          F6
'Cause you walked hand in hand

       G6   **C**
With another man in my place.

      Am Em   **Fmaj7 C6/9**
No re-ply,   no re-ply.

Norwegian Wood
(This Bird Has Flown)

Words and Music by John Lennon
and Paul McCartney

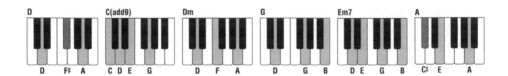

Intro ‖: D | | C(add9) G/B | D :‖

Verse 1

D
I once had a girl,

Or should I say

C(add9) G/B D
She once had me?

She showed me her room,

Isn't it good,

C(add9) G/B D
Norwe - gian wood?

Bridge 1

  Dm   **G**
She asked me to stay and she told me to sit anywhere.

  Dm   **Em7   A**
So I looked around and I noticed there wasn't a chair.

Verse 2

D
I sat on a rug

Biding my time,
C(add9) G/B D
Drinking her wine.

We talked until two,

And then she said,
C(add9) G/B D
"It's time for   bed."

Interlude

‖: D | | C(add9) G/B │D   :‖

Bridge 2

Dm   G
She told me she worked in the morning and started to laugh.
Dm   Em7 A
I told her I didn't and crawled off to sleep in the bath.

Verse 3

D
And when I awoke

I was alone,
C(add9) G/B D
This bird had flown.

So I lit a fire,

Isn't it good,
C(add9) G/B D
Norwe - gian wood?

Outro

│D | | C(add9) G/B│D

Not a Second Time

Words and Music by John Lennon
and Paul McCartney

Melody:

You know you made me cry.

Verse 1

    G   **E**
You know you made me cry.

    G   **E**
I see no use in wondering why,

  D   **G** **D7**
I cried for you.

Verse 2

    G   **E**
And now you've changed your mind,

    G   **E**
I see no reason to change mine.

  D   **Am**   **D**
My crying is through, oh.

Bridge 1

Am   **Bm**
You're giving me the same old line.

G   **Em**
I'm wondering why.

Am
You hurt me then, you're back again.

Bm   **D7**   **Em**
No, no, no, not a second time.

Solo		Am		Bm		G		Em		
		Am				Bm		D7		
		Em								

Verse 3

G   E
You know you made me cry.

G   E
I see no use in wondering why,

D   G   D7
I cried for you, _____ yeah.

Verse 4

Repeat Verse 2

Bridge 2

Repeat Bridge 1

Outro

N.C.   G   E
Not a second time.

            G   E
Not a second time.

            G E
No, no, no, no, no.   *Fade out*

Not Guilty

Words and Music by
George Harrison

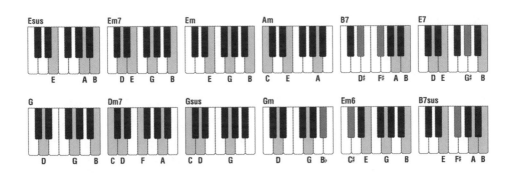

Intro |Esus   Em7 Em| |Esus   Em7 Em| |

Verse 1

      Am   Am/G   Am/F♯
Not guilty

   B7   **Em**
Of getting in your way,

        B7   **E7**
While you're trying to steal the day.

    Am   Am/G   Am/F♯
Not guilty,

    B7   **Em**
And I'm not before the rest.

    B7   **G   Dm7**
I'm not trying to steal your vest.

GUITAR CHORD SONGBOOK

Bridge 1

E7
　　I am not trying to be smart,

　　　　　　　　　Gsus　Gm
I only want what I can get.

　　　　　Em7　　　　Em6
I'm really sorry for your aging head,

　　B7sus　　　　　　B7
But like you heard me said,

Verse 2

　　　　Am　Am/G　Am/F♯
Not guilty.

　　　B7　　　　　Em
No use handing me a writ

　　　　B7　　　　　G　Dm7
While I'm trying to do my bit.

Bridge 2

E7
　　I don't expect to take your heart,

　　　　　　　　　Gsus　Gm
I only want what I can get.

　　　　Em7　　　　Em6
I'm really sorry that you're underfed,

　　B7sus　　　　B7
But like you heard me said,

Em　　　Em7　Esus　Em7　Em
Not guilty.

Solo

|Am Am/G | Am/F♯ | Em7 Em6| Em7 Em6|

|Am Am/G | Am/F♯ | Em7 Em6| Em7 Em6| Am/E Em|

Verse 3

       Am   Am/G   Am/F#
Not guilty

    B7   **Em**
For looking like a freak,

      B7   **E7**
Making friends with every Sikh.

      Am   Am/G   Am/F#
Not guilty,

    B7   **Em**
For leading you a-stray

      B7   **G   Dm7**
On the road to Manda-lay.

Bridge 3

E7
  I won't upset the apple cart,

                 Gsus Gm
I only want what I can get.

       Em7   **Em6**
I'm really sorry that you've been misled,

   B7sus   **B7**   **Am**
But like you heard me said, not guilty.

Outro

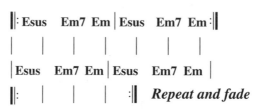

Ob-La-Di, Ob-La-Da

Words and Music by John Lennon
and Paul McCartney

Des-mond has a bar-row in the mar-ket place, _

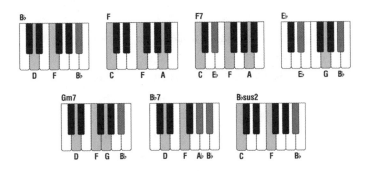

Intro |B♭ | | | |

Verse 1

B♭   F
Desmond has a barrow in the market place,

F7   B♭
Molly is a singer in a band.

                              E♭
Desmond says to Molly, girl, I like your face,

              B♭   F   B♭
And Molly says this as she takes him by the hand.

Chorus 1

              B♭   F Gm7
Ob-La-Di, Ob-La-Da, life goes on, bra,

B♭   F   B♭
La, la, how their life goes on.

                              F Gm7
Ob-La-Di, Ob-La-Da, life goes on, bra,

B♭   F   B♭
La, la, how their life goes on.

Verse 2

B♭   **F**
Desmond takes a trolley to the jeweler's store,

F7   **B♭**
Buys a twenty carat golden ring. (Ring.)

        E♭
Takes it back to Molly waiting at the door,

 B♭   **F**   **B♭**
As he gives it to her, she begins to sing:

Chorus 2   *Repeat Chorus 1*

       E♭
Bridge 1   In a couple of years,

            B♭ **B♭sus2** **B♭** **B♭7**
They have built a home sweet home.

E♭
 With a couple of kids running in the yard

 B♭/F   **F**
Of Desmond and Molly Jones.

      B♭   **F**
Verse 3   Happy ever after in the market place,

      F7   **B♭**
Desmond lets the children lend a hand.

         E♭
Molly stays at home and does her pretty face,

   B♭   **F**   **B♭**
And in the evening she still sings it with the band.

Chorus 3	*Repeat Chorus 1*
Bridge 2	*Repeat Bridge 1*

Verse 4

    B♭   **F**
Happy ever after in the market place,

    F7   **B♭**
Molly lets the children lend a hand.

                                   E♭
Desmond stays at home and does his pretty face,

        B♭   **F**   **B♭**
And in the evening she's a singer with the band.

Chorus 4

        B♭   **F** **Gm7**
Ob-La-Di, Ob-La-Da, life goes on, bra,

B♭   **F**   **B♭**
La, la, how their life goes on.

                    F **Gm7**
Ob-La-Di, Ob-La-Da, life goes on, bra,

B♭   **F**   **B♭**
La, la, how their life goes on.

And if you want some fun,

    F   **B♭**
Take Ob-La-Di-Bla-Da.

Nowhere Man

Words and Music by John Lennon
and Paul McCartney

Melody:

He's a real No - where _ Man,

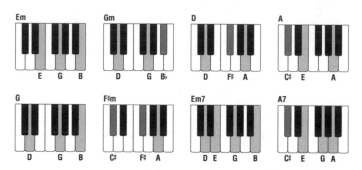

Verse 1

N.C.
He's a real Nowhere Man,

Sitting in his Nowhere Land,

Em   Gm   D
Making all his Nowhere plans for nobody.

Verse 2

D   A
Doesn't have a point of view.

G   D
Knows not where he's going to.

Em Gm   D
Isn't he a bit like you and me?

Bridge 1

F♯m   G
Nowhere Man, please listen.

F♯m   G
You don't know what you're missing.

F♯m Em7   A7
Nowhere Man, the world is at your command.

Solo	D	A	G	D	
	Em	Gm	D		

Verse 3

D   A
He's as blind as he can be.

G   D
Just sees what he wants to see.

Em   Gm   D
Nowhere Man, can you see me at all?

Bridge 2

F#m   G
Nowhere Man, don't worry.

F#m   G
Take your time, don't hurry.

F#m   Em7   A7
Leave it all till somebody else lends you a hand.

Verse 4   *Repeat Verse 2*

Bridge 3   *Repeat Bridge 1*

Verse 5

D   A
He's a real Nowhere Man,

G   D
Sitting in his Nowhere Land,

Em   Gm   D
Making all his Nowhere plans for nobody.

Em   Gm   D
Making all his Nowhere plans for nobody.

Em   Gm   D
Making all his Nowhere plans for nobody.

Octopus's Garden

Words and Music by
Richard Starkey

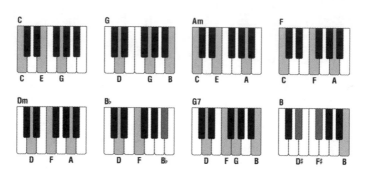

Intro |C G|C | |Am |F |G |

Verse 1

C   Am
I'd like to be   under the sea,

       F   G
In an octopus's garden in the shade.

C   Am
He'd let us in,   knows where we've been,

       F   G
In his octopus's garden in the shade.

Am   Am/G
I'd ask my friends to come and see

F   G
An octopus's garden with me.

Chorus 1

C   Am
I'd like to be   under the sea

       F   G   G
In an octopus's garden in the shade.

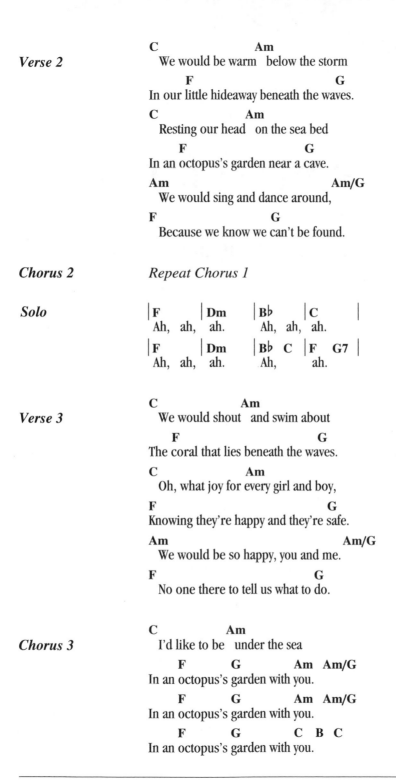

Verse 2

C   Am
We would be warm   below the storm
        F   G
In our little hideaway beneath the waves.
C   Am
Resting our head   on the sea bed
        F   G
In an octopus's garden near a cave.
Am   Am/G
We would sing and dance around,
F   G
Because we know we can't be found.

Chorus 2   *Repeat Chorus 1*

Solo | F | Dm | B♭ | C |
           Ah, ah, ah.   Ah, ah, ah.
          | F | Dm | B♭ C | F   G7 |
           Ah, ah, ah.   Ah,   ah.

Verse 3

C   Am
We would shout   and swim about
        F   G
The coral that lies beneath the waves.
C   Am
Oh, what joy for every girl and boy,
F   G
Knowing they're happy and they're safe.
Am   Am/G
We would be so happy, you and me.
F   G
No one there to tell us what to do.

Chorus 3

C   Am
I'd like to be   under the sea
        F   G   Am Am/G
In an octopus's garden with you.
        F   G   Am Am/G
In an octopus's garden with you.
        F   G   C B C
In an octopus's garden with you.

Oh! Darling

Words and Music by John Lennon
and Paul McCartney

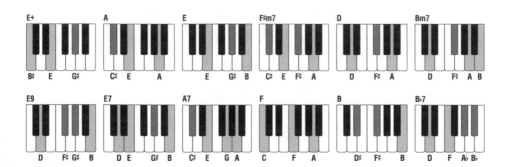

Intro | E+ |

Verse 1

     A   E
Oh! Darling, please be-lieve me,

F#m7   D
I'll never do you no harm.

    Bm7   E9
Be-lieve me when I tell you,

Bm7 E9   A   D A E7
I'll never do you no harm.

Verse 2

     A   E
Oh! Darling, if you leave me,

F#m7   D
I'll never make it a-lone.

    Bm7   E9
Be-lieve me when I beg you,

Bm7 E9   A   D A A7
Don't ever leave me a-lone.

Bridge 1

          D   F
When you told me you didn't need me anymore,

       A   A7
Well, you know I nearly broke down and cried.

       B
When you told me you didn't need me anymore,

       E   F   E N.C. E+
Well, you know I nearly broke down and died.

Verse 3

       A   E
Oh! Darling, if you leave me,

F#m7   D
I'll never make it a-lone.

   Bm7   E9
Be-lieve me when I tell   you,

Bm7   E9   A   D
I'll never do you no harm.

A   A7
(Believe me, darling.)

Bridge 2   *Repeat Bridge 1*

Verse 4

       A   E
Oh! Darling, please be-lieve me,

F#m7   D
I'll never let you down.

(Oh, believe me, darling.)

   Bm7   E9
Be-lieve me when I tell you,

Bm7   E9   A   D A Bb7 A7
 I'll never do you no harm.

Old Brown Shoe

Words and Music by
George Harrison

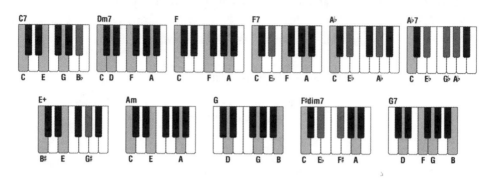

C7	Dm7	F	F7	A♭	A♭7
C E G B♭	C D F A	C F A	C E♭ F A	C E♭ A♭	C E♭ G♭ A♭

E+	Am	G	F#dim7	G7
B♯ E G♯	C E A	D G B	C E♭ F♯ A	D F G B

Intro 　　　|C7　　　|　　　|　　　|　　　|

Verse 1
　　　　　　　　C7
　　　　I want a love that's right,

　　　　But right is only half of what's wrong.

　　　　　　Dm7
　　　　I want a short-haired girl

　　　　Who sometimes wears it twice as long.

Chorus 1
　　　　　　　F　　　　F7
　　　　Now I'm stepping out this old brown shoe.
　　　　A♭　　　　A♭7
　　　　　Baby, I'm in love with you.
　　　　　F
　　　　I'm so glad you came here,
　　　　E+　　　　　　　　　Am　　C7
　　　　It won't be the same now, I'm telling you.

Verse 2

                  C7
You know, you pick me up from where

Some tried to drag me down.
           Dm7
And when I see your smile

Replacing every thoughtless frown.

Chorus 2

F   **F7**
  Got me escaping from this zoo.
A♭   A♭7
  Baby, I'm in love with you.
    F
I'm so glad you came here,
   E+   **Am**   **C7**
It won't be the same now, I'm telling you.

Bridge 1

 G
  If I grow up, I'll be a singer,
             F
Wearing rings   on every finger.
G
  Not worrying what they or you say.
                 F
I'll live and love and   maybe some day,
F♯dim7   **G**   **G7**
Who knows, baby, you may comfort me.

Solo

C7				
Dm7				
F	F7	A♭	A♭7	
F	E+	Am		

Bridge 2

      G
I may appear to be imperfect,

           F
My love is something you can't reject.

      G
I'm changing faster than the weather.

          F
If you and me should   get together,

F#dim7   **G**   **G7**
Who knows, baby, you may comfort me.

Verse 3

          C7
I want that love of yours,

To miss that love is something I'd hate.

        Dm7
I'll make an early start,

I'm making sure that I'm not late.

Chorus 3

   F   **F7**
For your sweet top lip I'm in the queue.

Ab   **Ab7**
Baby, I'm in love with you.

F
I'm so glad you came here,

  E+   **Am**
It won't be the same now when I'm with you.

   F
I'm so glad you came here,

  E+   **Am**
It won't be the same now that I'm with you.

Outro

‖: **C7** | | | :‖

‖: | | | :‖ *Repeat and fade*
Tu la,   tu ru tu. Tu la,   tu ru tu.

One After 909

Words and Music by John Lennon
and Paul McCartney

My ba - by says she's trav-'ling on the   one af - ter Nine - O - Nine. __

Intro ‖: **B7** | | :‖

Verse 1
B7
My baby says she's traveling

On the one after 909.

I said, "Move over, honey,

I'm traveling on that line."

Chorus 1
B7   **N.C.**
I said, "Move over once,

B7   **N.C.**
Move over twice,

E7
Come on baby, don't be cold as ice."

B7
 Said she's traveling

F♯7   **B7**
On the one after 909.

Verse 2	**B7**
	I begged her not to go,
	And I begged her on my bended knee.
	You're only fooling around,
	Only fooling around with me.

Chorus 2   *Repeat Chorus 1*

Bridge 1

E7   **B7**
  Pick up my bags,   run to the station.

C#7   **F#7**
Railman says, "You've got the wrong location."

E7   **B7**
  Pick up my bags,   run right home,

C#7   **F#7**
Then I find I've got the number wrong.

Verse 3

              B7
Well,   said she's traveling

On the one after 909.

I said, "Move over, honey,

I'm traveling on the line."

Chorus 3   *Repeat Chorus 1*

Interlude

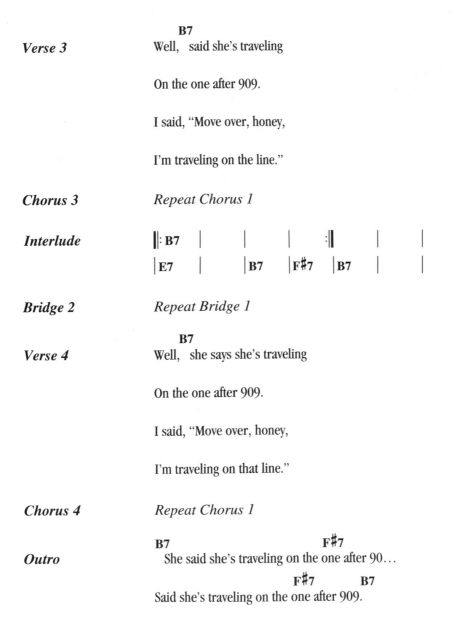

Bridge 2   *Repeat Bridge 1*

Verse 4

              B7
Well,   she says she's traveling

On the one after 909.

I said, "Move over, honey,

I'm traveling on that line."

Chorus 4   *Repeat Chorus 1*

Outro

B7   **F#7**
   She said she's traveling on the one after 90...

                        F#7   **B7**
Said she's traveling on the one after 909.

Only a Northern Song

Words and Music by
George Harrison

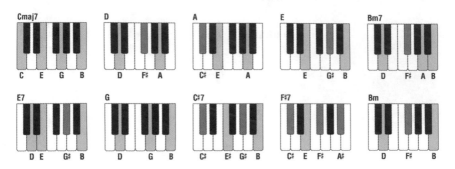

If you're lis - t'ning to ____ this song, __

Intro | Cmaj7 | D   A | E |

Verse 1

    A
  If you're listening to this song,

                                      Bm7
You may think the chords are going wrong.

        E7
But they're not,

             D
He just wrote it like that.

Verse 2

    A
  When you're listening late at night,

                                        Bm7
You may think the band are not quite right.

        E7
But they are,

            D
They just play it like that.

Chorus 1

```
E          Bm7       G      C#7
```
It doesn't really matter what chords I play,

```
    F#7
```
What words I say,

```
  Bm          F#7
```
Or time of day it is,

```
        D     A      E
```
'Cause it's only a Northern Song.

Interlude

| A | | | | Bm7 | |
| | E7 | | D | | |

Chorus 2

```
E          Bm7       G      C#7
```
It doesn't really matter what clothes I wear,

```
    F#7
```
Or how I fare,

```
  Bm          F#7
```
Or if my hair is brown,

```
        D     A      E
```
When it's only a Northern Song.

Verse 3

```
A
```
  If you think the harmony

```
                        Bm7
```
Is a little dark and out of key

```
        E7
```
You're cor-rect,

```
            D
```
There's nobody there.

| E Bm7 | G C#7 | F#7 | Bm7 | F#7 | |

```
        D          A      E
```
And I told you there's no one there.

Outro

A			Bm7		
E7		D		E Bm7	G C#7
F#7	Bm	F#7	D A	E		*Fade out*

Paperback Writer

Words and Music by John Lennon
and Paul McCartney

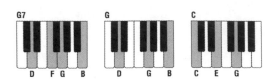

Intro

N.C.
Paperback writer... writer... writer.

|G7 | | | |

Verse 1

      G
Dear Sir or Madam, will you read my book?

It took me years to write, will you take a look?

It's based on a novel by a man named Lear,

And I need a job,

              C
So I want to be a paperback writer,

      G
Paperback writer.

	G
Verse 2	It's a dirty story of a dirty man,

And his clinging wife who doesn't understand.

His son is working for the Daily Mail.

It's a steady job,

        C
But he wants to be a paperback writer,

   G
Paperback writer.

N.C.   **G7**
(Paperback writer, paperback writer.)

   G
Verse 3   It's a thousand pages, give or take a few.

I'll be writing more in a week or two.

I can make it longer if you like the style,

I can change it 'round,

       C
And I want to be a paperback writer,

   G   **G7**
Paperback writer.

Verse 4	**G**
	If you really like it, you can have the rights.
	It could make a million for you overnight.
	If you must return it, you can send it here.
	But I need a break,
	C
	And I want to be a paperback writer,
	G
	Paperback writer.
	N.C. **G7**
	(Paperback writer, paperback writer.)

	G
Outro	‖: (Paperback writer, paperback writer.) :‖ ***Repeat and fade***

Penny Lane

Words and Music by John Lennon
and Paul McCartney

Pen-ny Lane, _ there is a bar - ber show-ing pho - to - graphs... _

Verse 1

                    B   C#m7   F#7
Penny Lane, there is a barber showing photographs

          B   Bm7
Of ev'ry head he's had the pleasure to know.

          G#m7♭5   Gmaj7
And all the people that come and go,

          F#7sus   F#7 F#7sus F#7
Stop and say hello.

Verse 2

                    B   C#m7   F#7
On the corner is a banker with a motorcar,

          B   Bm7
The little children laugh at him behind his back.

   G#m7♭5   Gmaj7
And the banker never wears a mac

   F#7sus   F#7 E
In the pouring rain.   Very strange.

Chorus 1

       A   A/C♯   D
Penny Lane is in my ears and in my eyes.

A   A/C♯   D
There beneath the blue suburban skies

      F♯7
I sit, and meanwhile back…

Verse 3

              B   C♯m7   F♯7
In Penny Lane there is a fireman with an hourglass,

              B   Bm7
And in his pocket is a portrait of the Queen.

      G♯m7♭5   Gmaj7
He likes to keep his fire engine clean.

      F♯7sus   F♯7 F♯7sus F♯7
It's a clean machine.

Solo

| B | C♯m7 F♯7 | B | Bm7 |

| G♯m7♭5 | Gmaj7 | F♯7sus F♯7 | E |

Chorus 2

       A   A/C♯   D
Penny Lane is in my ears and in my eyes.

A   A/C♯   D
  Full of fish and finger pies

         F♯7
In summer, meanwhile back…

Verse 4

        B   **C♯m7**   **F♯7**
Behind the shelter in the middle of the roundabout

        B   **Bm7**
The pretty nurse is selling poppies from a tray.

        G♯m7♭5   **Gmaj7**
And though she feels as if she's in a play,

      F♯7sus **F♯7** **F♯7sus** **F♯7**
She is anyway.

Verse 5

        B   **C♯m7**   **F♯7**
In Penny Lane the barber shaves another customer.

        B   **Bm7**
We see the banker sitting waiting for a trim.

        G♯m7♭5   **Gmaj7**
And then the fireman rushes in

      F♯7sus   **F♯7** **E**
From the pouring rain.   Very strange.

Chorus 3

        A   **A/C♯**   **D**
Penny Lane is in my ears and in my eyes.

  A   **A/C♯**   **D**
There beneath the blue suburban skies

      F♯7
I sit, and meanwhile back...

      B   **B/D♯**   **E**
Penny Lane is in my ears and in my eyes.

  B   **B/D♯**   **E**
There beneath the blue suburban skies...

        B
Penny Lane.

Piggies

Words and Music by
George Harrison

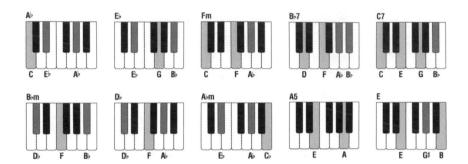

Intro | Ab Eb | Ab Eb |

Verse 1

Ab   Eb   Ab   Eb
Have you seen the little piggies crawling in the dirt?

Ab   Eb   Fm   Bb7
And for all the little piggies, life is getting worse,

Fm   Bb7   Eb   Ab Eb Ab Eb
Always having dirt to play around in.

Verse 2

Ab   Eb   Ab   Eb
Have you seen the bigger piggies in their starched white shirts?

Ab   Eb   Fm   Bb7
You will find the bigger piggies stirring up the dirt,

Fm   Bb7   Eb   Ab Eb Ab C7
Always have clean shirts to play around in.

Bridge

B♭m   C7
In their sties with all their backing,

D♭   A♭   E♭
They don't care what goes around.

B♭m   C7
In their eyes there's something lacking;

D♭   E♭
What they need's a damn good whacking!

Solo

| A♭   E♭ | A♭   E♭ | A♭   E♭ | Fm   B♭7 |

| Fm   B♭7 | E♭ | A♭   E♭ | A♭   E♭ |

Verse 3

A♭   E♭   A♭   E♭
Everywhere there's lots of piggies, living piggy lives.

A♭   E♭   Fm   B♭7
You can see them out for dinner with their piggy wives.

Fm   B♭7   E♭
Clutching forks and knives to eat their bacon.

Outro

| A♭   E♭ | A♭m   E♭ | A♭m   E♭ | B♭7   E♭ |

| N.C. | A5 | E
(One more time.)

Please Mr. Postman

Words and Music by Robert Bateman,
Georgia Dobbins, William Garrett,
Freddie Gorman and Brian Holland

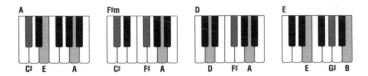

Intro

    A
Oh, yes, wait a minute, Mr. Postman.

F♯m
  Wait, Mr. Postman.

Chorus 1

    A
  Mr. Postman, look and see.

F♯m
  Is there a letter in your bag for me?

D
  I've been a waiting a long, long time

E
  Since I heard from that gal of mine.

Verse 1

A
There must be some word today

F♯m
From my girlfriend so far away.

D
Please, Mr. Postman, look and see

E
If there's a letter, a letter for me.

A
I've been standin' here waiting, Mr. Postman,

F♯m
So patiently

D
For just a card, or just a letter

E
Saying she's returning home to me.

Chorus 2　　*Repeat Chorus 1*

Verse 2

A
So many days you've passed me by,

F♯m
See the tears standin' in my eyes.

D
You didn't stop to make me feel better

E
By leaving me a card or a letter.

Chorus 3　　*Repeat Chorus 1*

Outro

　　　　　　A
‖: You gotta wait a minute, wait a minute, oh yeah.

F♯m
Wait a minute, wait a minute, oh yeah.

　　　　　　D
You gotta wait a minute, wait a minute, oh yeah.

E
Check it and see. One more time for me. :‖　***Repeat and fade***

Please Please Me

Words and Music by John Lennon
and Paul McCartney

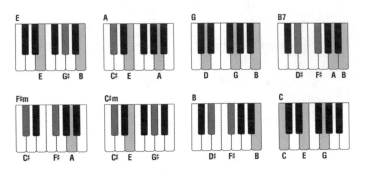

Intro | E | | | |

Verse 1

E   A E G A B7
Last night I said these words to my girl:

E   A E
I know you never even try, girl.

Chorus 1

    A F#m
Come on, come on.

   C#m A
Come on, come on.

    E   A
Please, please me, whoa yeah,

   B7 E A B
Like I please you.

Verse 2

E   A E G A B7
You don't need me to show the way, love.

E   A E
Why do I always have to say, love.

Chorus 2

    A   F♯m
Come on, come on.

     C♯m   A
Come on, come on.

     E   A
Please, please me, whoa yeah,

    B7   E A B
Like I please you.

Bridge

A
I don't want to sound complaining,

B7   E
But you know there's always rain in my heart.

A
I do all the pleasing with you,

B7   E
It's so hard to reason with you.

    A   B7   E   A B
Oh yeah, why do you make me blue?

Verse 3   *Repeat Verse 1*

Chorus 3

    A   F♯m
Come on, come on.

     C♯m   A
Come on, come on.

     E   A
Please, please me, whoa yeah,

    B7
Like I please you.

E   A
Please, please me, whoa yeah,

    B7
Like I please you.

E   A
Please, please me, whoa yeah,

    B7   E G C B7 E
Like I please you.

Polythene Pam

Words and Music by John Lennon
and Paul McCartney

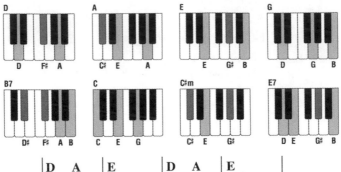

Well, you should see   Pol - y-thene   Pam.

Intro |D   A |E |D   A |E |

Verse 1
                 D A   E
Well, you should see Polythene Pam.
                      D   A   E
She's so good looking, but she looks like a man.
                   G   B7
Well, you should see her in drag, dressed in her polythene bag.
                 D A   E
Yes, you should see Polythene Pam.
C   D   E   D A E D A E
Yeah, yeah, yeah.

Verse 2
                 D   A   E
Get a dose of her in jackboots and kilt.
                     D   A   E
She's a killer diller when she's dressed to the hilt.
                G   B7
She's the kind of a girl that makes the News of the World,
                   C   D   E
Yes, you could say she was at-tractively built.
C   D   E   D A E D A E
Yeah, yeah, yeah.

Solo ‖: D   A |E |D   A |E   :‖ *Play 4 times*

     | | | |D |C♯m |E7/B
                                              Oh, look out!

Revolution

Words and Music by John Lennon
and Paul McCartney

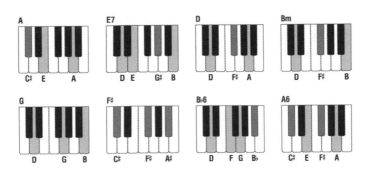

Intro | A | | | | E7 | |

Verse 1

        A
You say you want a revolution,

            D
Well, you know,

                  A
We all want to change the world.

You tell me that it's evolution,

            D
Well, you know,

                  E7
We all want to change the world.

Bm/F#   E7
But when you talk about destruction,

Bm/F#   G   A F#
Don't you know that you can count me out?

	E7 A D
Chorus 1	Don't you know it's going to be al-right?

A   D   A   D   E7
Al-right,   al-right.

Verse 2	A You say you got a real solution,

         D
Well, you know,

               A
We'd all love to see the plan.

You ask me for a contribution,

         D
Well, you know,

               E7
We're all doing what we can.

Bm/F♯   E7
But if you want money for people with minds that hate,

Bm/F♯   G   A F♯
All I can tell you is, brother, you'll have to wait.

Chorus 2   *Repeat Chorus 1*

Solo |A | | |D | | |

                    |E7 | | | | |

Verse 3

       A
You say you'll change the Constitution,

         D
Well, you know,

             A
We all want to change your head.

You tell me it's the institution,

         D
Well, you know,

              E7
You'd better free your mind in-stead.

Bm/F♯   **E7**
  But if you go carrying pictures of Chairman Mao,

Bm/F♯   **G A F♯**
  You ain't gonna make it with anyone an - y - how.

Chorus 3   *Repeat Chorus 1*

       A   **D**
Outro   Al-right, al-right,

       A   **D**
Al-right, al-right,

       A   **D**
Al-right, al-right,

       E7   **B♭6 A6**
Al-right, alright!

P.S. I Love You

Words and Music by John Lennon
and Paul McCartney

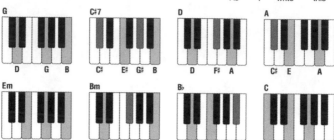

Intro

    G C#7   D
As I write this letter,

    G   C#7   D
Send my love to you.

      G   C#7   D
Re-member that I'll always

         A   D
Be in love with you.

Verse 1

    D   Em   D
Treasure these few words till we're to-gether:

    A   Bm
Keep all my love for-ever.

    A   B♭
P.S. I love you,

      C D
You, you, you.

Verse 2

    D   Em   D
I'll be coming home again to you, love.

     A   Bm
Un-til the day I do, love,

    A   B♭
P.S. I love you,

      C D
You, you, you.

Bridge 1	G D

Bridge 1

G D
As I write this letter,

G   D
Send my love to you,

 G   D
Re-member that I'll always

  A D
Be in love with you.

Verse 3

Repeat Verse 1

Bridge 2

G   D
As I write this letter, (Oh.)

G   D
Send my love to you, (You know I want you to.)

 G   D
Re-member that I'll always, yeah,

  A   D
Be in love with you.

Verse 4

D   Em   D
I'll be coming home again to you, love.

  A   Bm
Until the day I do, love,

A   B♭
P.S. I love you,

  C D
You, you, you.

B♭ C D
You, you, you.

B♭ C D
I love you.

Rain

Words and Music by John Lennon
and Paul McCartney

Melody:

If the rain comes, they run and hide their heads.

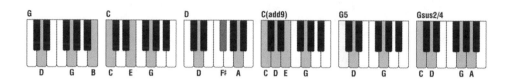

G   C   D   C(add9)   G5   Gsus2/4

D   G   B   C   E   G   D   F♯   A   C   D   E   G   D   G   C   D   G   A

Intro | G | | | |

Verse 1
       G
If the rain comes,

       C   **D**   **G**
They run and hide their heads.

       C   **D**   **G**
They might as well be ___ dead,

       C(add9)   **G**
If the rain comes, if the rain comes.

Verse 2
       G
When the sun shines,

       C   **D**   **G**
They slip into the shade,

       C   **D**   **G**
And sip their lemonade,

       C(add9)   **G**
When the sun shines, when the sun shines.

	G5 Gsus2/4 G5

Chorus 1

G5   Gsus2/4   G5
Rain, _____ I don't mind.

G5   Gsus2/4   G5
Shine, _____ the weather's fine.

Verse 3

       G
I can show you

     C   D   G
That when it starts to rain,

C   D   G
Everything's the same.

     C(add9)   G
I can show you, I can show you.

Chorus 2

Repeat Chorus 1

Verse 4

      G
Can you hear me

C   D   G
That when it rains and ____ shines,

    C   D   G
It's just a state of mind?

      C(add9)
Can you hear me?

      G
Can you hear me?

Outro

‖: G | | | :‖   *Repeat and fade*

Revolution 1

Words and Music by John Lennon
and Paul McCartney

You say you want a rev-o-lu-tion, _____

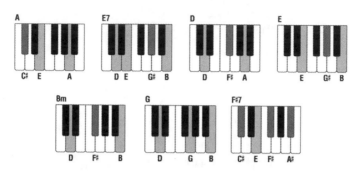

Intro |**A** | | |**E7** |

Verse 1
           A
You say you want a revolution,

           D
Well, you know,

                A
We all want to change the world.

You tell me that it's evolution,

           D
Well, you know,

              E
We all want to change the world.

Bm   **E**
  But when you talk about de-struction,

Bm   **G**   **A** **F#7** **E**
  Don't you know that you can count me out, in?

Chorus 1	**A** **D** Don't you know it's gonna be al-right?

Chorus 1

              A   **D**
Don't you know it's gonna be al-right?

              A   **D**
Don't you know it's gonna be al-right?

              A   **D**   **E7**
Don't you know it's gonna be al-right?

Verse 2

      A
You say you got a real solution,

       D
Well, you know,

           A
We'd all love to see the plan.

(Ba, oh, shoo, be, doo, wop.)

(Ba, oh, shoo, be, doo, wop.)

You ask me for a contribution,

       D
Well, you know,

             E
We all do it when we can.

Bm   **E**
  But if you want money for people with minds that hate,

Bm   **G**   **A** **F$\sharp$7** **E**
  All I can tell you is, brother, you have to wait.

Chorus 2   *Repeat Chorus 1*

Verse 3

        A
You say you'll change the Constitution,
        D
Well, you know,
                A
We'd all love to change your head.

(Ba, oh, shoo, be, doo, wop.)

(Ba, oh, shoo, be, doo, wop.)

You tell me it's the institution,
        D
Well, you know,
                E
You'd better free your mind in-stead.

(Ba, oh, shoo, be, doo, wop.)

(Ba, oh, shoo, be, doo, wop.)
Bm   **E**
  But if you go carrying pictures of Chairman Mao,
Bm   **G A F♯7 E**
  You ain't gonna make it with anyone an - y - how.

Chorus 3   *Repeat Chorus 1*

        A
Outro   (Oh, shoo, be, doo, wop.)
        D
  Ah, ah, ah, ah.
        A   **D**
  Ah, ah, ah, ah.
              A
Ah, ah, al - right.
      D   **A**
Alright, al-right.
           D
Alright, al-right.
          A
Alright, al-right!
‖: **A** | **D**   :‖ *Repeat and fade*

Rocky Racoon

Words and Music by John Lennon
and Paul McCartney

Rock - y Rac - coon ___ checked in - to his room, ___

Intro |Am7 | |

Verse 1
        Am7
Now somewhere in the black mountain hills of Dakota

          D7sus   **D7**
There lived a young boy named Rocky Rac-coon.

G7   **C**
And one day his woman ran off with another guy,

C/B   **Am7**
Hit young Rocky in the eye.

Rocky didn't like that,

         D7sus   **D7**
He said, "I'm gonna get that boy."

      G7
So one day he walked into town,

                       C   **C/B**
Booked himself a room in the local saloon.

Verse 2

Am7   D7sus   D7
Rocky Raccoon checked into his room,

G7   C C/B
Only to find Gideon's Bi-ble.

Am7   D7sus   D7
Rocky had come, e-quipped with a gun,

 G7   C C/B
To shoot off the legs of his rival.

  Am7   D7sus   D7
His rival, it seems, had broken his dreams,

 G7   C C/B
By stealing the girl of his fancy.

  Am7   D7sus   D7
Her name was Magill, and she called herself Lil,

 G7   C   C/B
But everyone knew her as Nancy.

Verse 3

  Am7   D7sus   D7
Now she and her man, who called himself Dan,

  G7   C   C/B
Were in the next room at the hoedown.

Am7   D7sus   D7
Rocky burst in, and grinning a grin,

    G7   C   C/B
He said, "Danny boy, this is a show-down."

  Am7   D7sus   D7
But Daniel was hot, he drew first and shot,

 G7   C   C/B
And Rocky collapsed in the corner.

Solo ‖: Am7 | D7sus D7 | G7 | C C/B :‖

Verse 4

       Am7   D7sus   D7
Now, the doctor came in, stinking of gin,

     G7   C C/B
And pro-ceeded to lie on the table.

      Am7
He said, "Rocky, you met your match,"

     D7sus   D7
And Rocky said, "Doc, it's only a scratch,

     G7
And I'll be better, I'll be better, Doc,

        C   C/B
As soon as I am   able."

Verse 5

    Am7   D7sus   D7
Now Rocky Raccoon, he fell back in his room,

G7   C C/B
Only to find Gideon's Bi-ble.

Am7   D7sus   D7
Gideon checked out and left in no doubt

   G7   C C/B
To help with good Rocky's revival.

Outro | Am7 | D7sus D7 | G7 | C C/B |
| Am7 | D7sus D7 |
(Come on, Rocky boy.)   (Come on, Rocky boy.)
| G7 | C G7 | C

Run for Your Life

Words and Music by John Lennon
and Paul McCartney

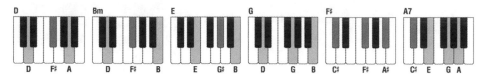

Intro | D | | |

Verse 1
      D
Well, I'd rather see you dead, little girl,

      Bm
Than to be with another man.

      D
You'd better keep your head, little girl,

      Bm
Or I won't know where I am.

Chorus 1
      Bm   **E**
You'd better run for your life if you can, little girl.

Bm   **E**
Hide your head in the sand, little girl.

Bm   **G**
Catch you with another man,

F♯   **Bm**   **D**
That's the end, little girl.

Verse 2
      D
Well, you know that I'm a wicked guy

      Bm
And I was born with a jealous mind.

      D
And I can't spend my whole life trying

      Bm
Just to make you toe the line.

Chorus 2	*Repeat Chorus 1*

Solo | D | | G | D | A7 | D | |

D
Verse 3   Let this be a sermon;

      Bm
I mean everything I said.

D
Baby, I'm determined,

      Bm
And I'd rather see you dead.

Chorus 3   *Repeat Chorus 1*

      D
Verse 4   I'd rather see you dead, little girl,

      Bm
Than to be with another man.

      D
You'd better keep your head, little girl,

     Bm
Or you won't know where I am.

      Bm   **E**
Chorus 4   You'd better run for your life if you can, little girl.

Bm   **E**
Hide your head in the sand, little girl.

Bm   **G**
Catch you with another man,

F♯   **Bm**
That's the end, little girl.

   | D | ‖:   :‖ *Repeat and fade*
         Na, na, na.   Na, na.

Savoy Truffle

Words and Music by
by George Harrison

Creme tan - ge - rine and mon-tel - i - mar, —

Intro | E7 | |

Verse 1

N.C.   E7
Cream tanger-ine and montelimar,

F♯   A
A ginger sling with a pineapple heart.

G   B
A coffee dessert, yes, you know it's good news.

Chorus 1

                   Em   Em(add♭6) Em6
But you'll have to have them all pulled out

            Em(add♭6) C G E7
After the Savoy   truf-fle.

Verse 2

N.C.   E7
Cool cherry cream, nice apple tart.

F♯   A
I feel your taste all the time we're a-part,

G   B
Coconut fudge really blows down those blues.

Chorus 2

                   Em   Em(add♭6) Em6
But you'll have to have them all pulled out

            Em(add♭6) C G
After the Savoy   truf-fle.

	Em	**A**
Bridge 1	You might not feel it now,	

                       Asus   **A**
But when the pain cuts through,

                    G   **B**
You're going to know, and how.

              Em   **A**
The sweat is gonna fill your head.

                   Asus   **A**   **G**   **B**
When it becomes too much, you'll shout a-loud…

Solo

	E7				**F♯**	
	A		**G**		**B**	

Chorus 3   *Repeat Chorus 2*

              Em   **A**
Bridge 2   You know that what you eat you are,

                  Asus **A**   **G B**
But what is sweet now turns so sour.

              Em   **A**
We all know Ob-la-di-bla-da,

                  Asus A   **G**   **B**
But can you show me where you are?

Verse 3   *Repeat Verse 1*

               Em   **Em(add♭6) Em6**
Chorus 4   But you'll have to have them all pulled out

                  Em(add♭6) **C**   **G**
After the Savoy   truf-fle.

               Em   **Em(add♭6) Em6**
But you'll have to have them all pulled out

                  Em(add♭6) **C**   **G**
After the Savoy   truf-fle.

Sexy Sadie

Words and Music by John Lennon
and Paul McCartney

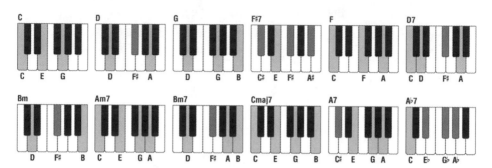

Intro

| C   D | G   F#7 | F   D7 |

Verse 1

G   F#7 Bm
Sexy Sa-die, what have you done?

C   D   G F#7
You made a fool of everyone.

C   D   G F#7
You made a fool of everyone.

     F   D7   G
Sexy Sadie, oh, what have you done?

Verse 2

G   F#7 Bm
Sexy Sa-die, you broke the rules.

C   D   G F#7
You laid it down for all to see.

C   D   G F#7
You laid it down for all to see.

     F   D7   G
Sexy Sadie, oh, you broke the rules.

Bridge 1

G   Am7   Bm Cmaj7
One sunny day the world was waiting,

G   Am7   Bm7 C
She came along to turn on everyone.

    A7   Ab7   G
Sexy Sa-die, the greatest of them all.

Verse 3

G   F#7 Bm
Sexy Sa-die, how did you know?

C   D   G F#7
The world was waiting just for you.

C   D   G F#7
The world was waiting just for you.

    F   D7   G
Sexy Sadie, oh, how did you know?

Verse 4

G   F#7 Bm
Sexy Sa-die, you'll get yours yet.

C   D G F#7
However big you think you are.

C   D   G F#7
However big you think you are.

    F   D7   G
Sexy Sadie, oh, you'll get yours yet.

Bridge 2

G   Am7   Bm7 Cmaj7
We gave her everything we owned just to sit at her table.

G   Am7   Bm7 C
Just a smile would light-en everything.

    A7   Ab7   G F#7
Sexy Sa-die, she's the latest and the greatest of them all.

Outro

‖: Bm7 |C   D |G   F#7 |
   Ooh.

|C   D |G   F#7 |
She made a fool of everyone.

|F   D7 |G   F#7 :‖ *Repeat and fade*
   Sexy Sadie.

Sgt. Pepper's Lonely Hearts Club Band

Words and Music by John Lennon
and Paul McCartney

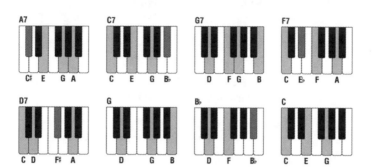

Intro |A7 | |C7 |G7 |

Verse 1

          G7   **A7**
It was twenty years ago to-day,

           C7   **G7**
Sergeant Pepper taught the band to play.

                    A7
They've been going in and out of style,

         C7   **G7**
But they're guaranteed to raise a smile.

   A7
So may I introduce to you

   C7
The act you've known for all these years:

G7   **C7**   **G7**
Sergeant Pepper's Lonely Hearts Club Band.

Interlude |C7 |F7 |C7 |D7 | | |

Chorus

                      G   B♭   C7   G
We're Sergeant Pepper's Lonely Hearts Club Band,

        C7   G7
We hope you will enjoy the show.

G   B♭   C7   G
Sergeant Pepper's Lonely Hearts Club Band,

      A7   D7
Sit back and let the evening go.

C7   G7
Sergeant Pepper's Lonely, Sergeant Pepper's Lonely,

A7   C7   G7
Sergeant Pepper's Lonely Hearts Club Band.

          C7
Bridge   It's wonderful to be here,

        F7
It's certainly a thrill.

          C7
You're such a lovely audience,

        D7
We'd like to take you home with us,

We'd love to take you home.

          N.C.   G7   A7
Verse 2   I don't really want to stop the show,

        C7   G7
But I thought you might like to know,

                                        A7
That the singer's going to sing a song,

        C7   G7
And he wants you all to sing a-long.

      A7
So let me introduce to you

      C7
The one and only Billy Shears,

        G7   C7   G7   C
And Sergeant Pepper's Lonely Hearts Club Band, yeah!

Sgt. Pepper's Lonely Hearts Club Band

(Reprise)

Words and Music by John Lennon
and Paul McCartney

Melody:

We're Ser-geant Pep-per's Lone - ly Hearts __ Club Band,

F Ab Bb G

C F A C Eb Ab D F Bb D G B

C D A

C E G D F# A C# E A

Intro | *Drums for 4 bars* | F | | | |

Verse 1

     F   Ab   Bb   F
We're Sergeant Pepper's Lonely Hearts Club Band,

  Bb   F
We hope you have enjoyed the show.

      Ab   Bb   F
Sergeant Pepper's Lonely Hearts Club Band,

    G   C
We're sorry, but it's time to go.

Bb   F
 Sergeant Pepper's Lonely, Sergeant Pepper's Lonely,

G   D
Sergeant Pepper's Lonely, Sergeant Pepper's Lonely.

Verse 2

    G   Bb   C   G
Ser-geant Pepper's Lonely Hearts Club Band,

    C   G
We'd like to thank you once a-gain.

    G   Bb   C   G
Ser-geant Pepper's one and only Lonely Hearts Club Band,

    A   D
It's getting very near the end.

    C   G
Ser-geant Pepper's Lonely, Ser-geant Pepper's Lonely,

    A   C   G Bb C G
Ser-geant Pepper's Lonely Hearts Club Band.

She Loves You

Words and Music by John Lennon
and Paul McCartney

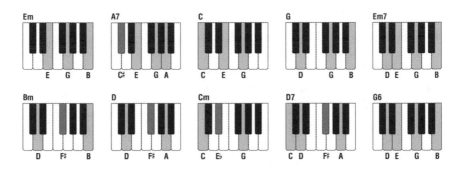

Intro

Em
She loves you, yeah, yeah, yeah.

A7
She loves you, yeah, yeah, yeah.

C   **G**
She loves you, yeah, yeah, yeah, yeah.

Verse 1

G   **Em7**
You think you lost your love,

Bm   **D**
Well, I saw her yester-day.

G   **Em7**
It's you she's thinking of,

Bm   **D**
And she told me what to say.

G   **Em**
She says she loves you, and you know that can't be bad.

Cm   **D**
Yes, she loves you, and you know you should be glad.

Verse 2

        G   **Em7**
She said you hurt her so,

        Bm   **D**
She almost lost her mind.

        G   **Em7**
But now she says she knows,

          Bm   **D**
You're not the hurting kind.

               G   **Em**
She says she loves you, and you know that can't be bad.

           Cm   **D**
Yes, she loves you, and you know you should be glad. Ooh.

Chorus 1

        Em
She loves you, yeah, yeah, yeah.

        A7
She loves you, yeah, yeah, yeah.

        Cm
With a love like that,

        D7   **G**
You know you should be glad.

Verse 3

       G   **Em7**
You know it's up to you,

  Bm   **D**
I think it's only fair.

G   **Em7**
Pride can hurt you too,

  Bm   **D**
A-pologize to her.

              G   **Em**
Because she loves you, and you know that can't be bad.

          Cm   **D**
Yes, she loves you, and you know you should be glad. Ooh.

Chorus 2

       Em
She loves you, yeah, yeah, yeah.

       A7
She loves you, yeah, yeah, yeah.

       Cm
With a love like that,

       D7   **G**   **Em**
You know you should be glad.

       Cm   **N.C.**
With a love like that,

       D   **G**   **Em**
You know you should be glad.

       Cm   **N.C.**
With a love like that,

       D7   **G**
You know you should be glad.

Em
  Yeah, yeah, yeah.

C   **G6**
Yeah, yeah, yeah, yeah.

She Came in Through the Bathroom Window

Words and Music by John Lennon
and Paul McCartney

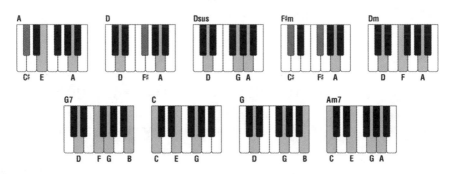

				A	D	Dsus	D

Verse 1

      A   **D**   **Dsus** **D**
She came in through the bathroom win-dow,

      A   **F#m**   **D** **Dsus** **D**
Protected by a silver spoon.

      A   **F#m**   **D** **Dsus**
But now she sucks her thumb and won-ders

         D
By the banks of her own lagoon.

Bridge 1

      A   **Dm**
Didn't anybody tell her?

      A   **Dm**
Didn't anybody see?

      G7   **C** **G/B** **Am7**
Sunday's on the phone to Mon-day,

      G7   **C**   **A**
Tuesday's on the phone to me.

PIANO CHORD SONGBOOK

Verse 2

```
        A                          D  Dsus  D
        She said she'd always been a danc-er,

        A           F#m          D  Dsus  D
        She worked at fifteen clubs a day.

        A           F#m              D    Dsus
        And though she thought I knew the answer,

              D
        Well, I knew what I could not say.
```

Verse 3

```
        A                        D     Dsus  D
        And so I quit the police de-partment,

        A         F#m        D  Dsus  D
        And got my-self a steady job.

        A           F#m              D    Dsus
        And though she tried her best to help me,

              D
        She could steal, but she could not rob.
```

Bridge 2

```
        A            Dm
        Didn't anybody tell her?

        A              Dm
        Didn't anybody see?

        G7                          C   G/B  Am7
        Sunday's on the phone to Mon-day,

        G7                      C
        Tuesday's on the phone to me.

              A
        Oh, yeah.
```

She Said She Said

Words and Music by John Lennon
and Paul McCartney

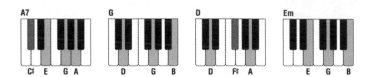

Intro | A7 | | |

Verse 1
A7   G   D
She said,

              A7   G   D
"I know what it's like to be dead.

            A7   G   D
I know what it is to be sad."

        A7   G   D   A7
And she's making me feel like I've never been born.

| G7 | D   A7 |

Verse 2
A7   G   D
I said,

           A7   G   D
"Who put all those things in your head?

           A7   G   D
Things that make me feel that I'm mad,

        A7   G   D   A7
And you're making me feel like I've never been born."

| G | D   A7 |

Bridge 1

A7   G   A7
She said, "You don't under-stand what I said."

      G   A7
I said, "No, no, no, you're wrong.

           Em A7
When I was a boy

          D A7   D
Everything was right,   everything was right."

Verse 3

A7   G D
I said,

          A7   G   D
"Even though you know what you know,

          A7   G   D
I know that I'm ready to leave,

          A7   G   D   A7
'Cause you're making me feel like I've never been born."

| G |D A7 |

Bridge 2   *Repeat Bridge 1*

Verse 4   *Repeat Verse 3*

Outro

A7
She said, (She said.)

"I know what it's like to be dead."

(I know what it's like to be dead.)

"I know what it's like to be sad."

(I know what it's like to be sad.)

"I know what it's like to be dead."   ***Fade out***

She's a Woman

Words and Music by John Lennon
and Paul McCartney

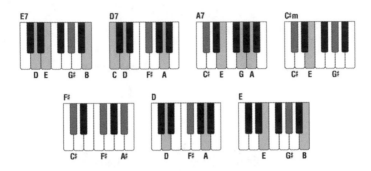

Intro |E7 | |D7 | |A7 | | | | |

Verse 1

    A7   D7   A7
My love don't give me presents,

            D7   A7
I know that she's no peasant.

D7
Only ever has to give me love forever and forever.

    A7   D7   A7
My love don't give me presents,

E7
Turn me on when I get lonely.

D7   A7
People tell me that she's only foolin',

    D7   A7   E7
I know she isn't.

Verse 2

A7   D7   A7
She don't give boys the eye,

        D7   A7
She hate to see me cry.

D7
She is happy just to hear me say that I will never leave her.

A7   D7   A7
She don't give boys the eye,

E7
She will never make me jealous.

D7   A7
Give me all her time as well as lovin',

    D7   A7
Don't ask me why.

Bridge 1

C#m   F#
She's a woman who understands,

C#m   D   E
She's a woman who loves her man.

Verse 3

Repeat Verse 1

Interlude

| A7 | | | | D7 | | |
| A7 | | E7 | D7 | A7 | E7 | |

Bridge 2

Repeat Bridge 1

Verse 4

A7   D7   A7
My love don't give me presents,

        D7   A7
I know that she's no peasant.

D7
Only ever has to give me love forever and forever.

    A7   D7   A7
My love don't give me presents,

E7
Turn me on when I get lonely.

D7   A7
People tell me that she's only foolin',

    D7   A7
I know she isn't.

She's a woman, she's a woman,

        D7   A7
She's a woman, she's a woman…   ***Fade out***

She's Leaving Home

Words and Music by John Lennon
and Paul McCartney

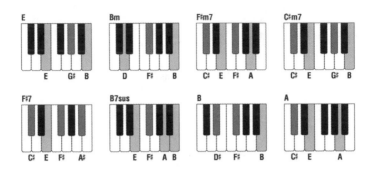

Intro | E | | | |

Verse 1

E   Bm   F#m7   C#m7   F#7
Wednesday morning at five o'clock, as the day begins,

B7sus   B
Silently closing her bedroom door,

B7sus   B
Leaving the note that she hoped would say more.

Verse 2

           E   Bm   F#m7   C#m7   F#7
She goes down-stairs to the kitchen clutching her handkerchief.

B7sus   B
Quietly turning the back door key,

B7sus   B
Stepping outside she is free.

Chorus 1

E
She (We gave her most of our lives.)

Is leaving (Sacrificed most of our lives.)

       Bm/D   (C♯m7)
Home. (We gave her everything money could buy.)

C♯m7   F♯7
She's leaving home after living alone (Bye, bye.)

   C♯m7   F♯7
For so many years.

Verse 3

E   Bm   F♯m7   C♯m7   F♯7
Father snores as his wife gets into her dressing gown.

B7sus   B
Picks up the letter that's lying there,

B7sus   B
Standing alone at the top of the stairs.

Verse 4

     E   Bm   F♯m7
She breaks down and cries to her husband,

    C♯m7   F♯7
"Daddy, our baby's gone!"

B7sus   B
"Why would she treat us so thoughtlessly?

B7sus   B
How could she do this to me?"

Chorus 2

      E
She (We never thought of ourselves.)

Is leaving (Never a thought for ourselves.)

                  Bm/D   **(C#m7)**
Home. (We've struggled hard all our lives to get by.)
C#m7   **F#7**
She's leaving home after living alone (Bye, bye.)
      C#m7   **F#7**
For so many years.

Verse 5

E   **Bm**   **F#m7**   **C#m7**   **F#7**
Friday morning at nine o'clock, she is far away.

B7sus   **B**
Waiting to keep the appointment she made,

B7sus   **B**
Meeting a man from the motor trade.

Chorus 3

E
She (What did we do that was wrong?)

Is having (We didn't know it was wrong.)

                 Bm/D   **(C#m7)**
Fun. (Fun is the one thing that money can't buy.)
C#m7   **F#7**
Something inside that was always denied (Bye, bye.)
      C#m7   **F#7**
For so many years.
C#m7   **F#7**
She's leaving home.

      A   **E**
(Bye, bye.)

Strawberry Fields Forever

Words and Music by John Lennon
and Paul McCartney

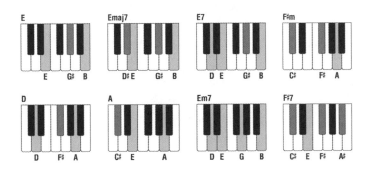

Intro |E   Emaj7| E7 |F#m E |D   A |

Chorus 1

A
Let me take you down,

            Em7
'Cause I'm going to

Strawberry Fields.

F#7
Nothing is real,

    D   F#7
And nothing to get hung about.

D   A
Strawberry Fields for-ever.

Verse 1

E   Emaj7   E7
Living is easy with eyes closed,

F#m   E   D
  Misunder-standing all you see.

          E   A
It's getting hard to be some-one,

         F#m
But it all works out;

D   E   D A
  It doesn't matter much to me.

Chorus 2   *Repeat Chorus 1*

Verse 2

E   Emaj7   E7
No one I think is in my tree,

F#m   E   D
  I mean, it must be high or low.

        E   A
That is, you can't, you know, tune in,

        F#m
But it's all right.

D   E   D   A
  That is, I think it's not too bad.

Chorus 3   *Repeat Chorus 1*

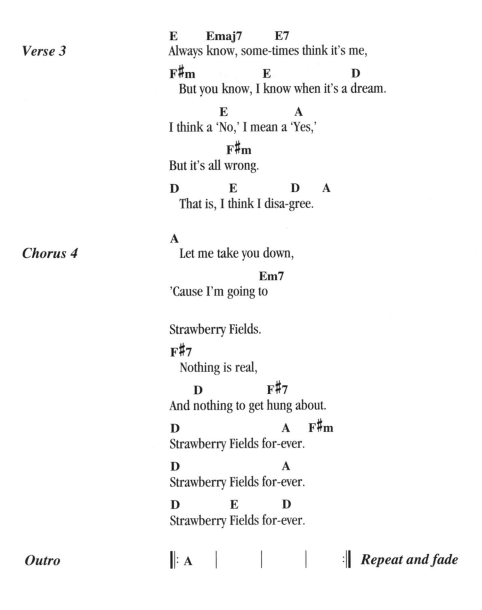

Verse 3

    E   Emaj7   E7
Always know, some-times think it's me,

F#m   E   D
But you know, I know when it's a dream.

          E   A
I think a 'No,' I mean a 'Yes,'

        F#m
But it's all wrong.

D   E   D   A
  That is, I think I disa-gree.

Chorus 4

A
  Let me take you down,

                Em7
'Cause I'm going to

Strawberry Fields.

F#7
  Nothing is real,

     D   F#7
And nothing to get hung about.

D   A F#m
Strawberry Fields for-ever.

D   A
Strawberry Fields for-ever.

D   E   D
Strawberry Fields for-ever.

Outro   ‖: A | | | :‖ *Repeat and fade*

Slow Down

Words and Music by
Larry Williams

Well, come on, pret-ty ba-by, won't ya walk with me? __

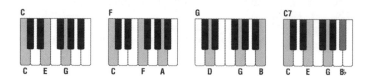

Intro

C								
F				C				
G		F		C				

Verse 1

        C
Well, come on, pretty baby, won't ya walk with me?

Come on, pretty baby, won't ya talk with me?

Come on, pretty baby, give me one more chance,
N.C.
  Try and save our romance.

       F
Slow down,

               C
Baby, now you're movin' way too fast.

     G   **F**
You gotta gimme little lovin', gimme little lovin',

C N.C.   **C**
  Ow, if you want our love to last.

Verse 2

               C
Well, I used to walk you home, baby, after school,

Carry your books home, too.

But now you don't care a dime for me,

    N.C.
Ba-by, what you try'n' to do?

         F
You better slow down.

                      C
Baby, now you're movin' way too fast.

        G   F
You gotta gimme little lovin', gimme little lovin',

C N.C.   C
  Ow, if you want our love to last.

Solo   *Repeat Intro*

Verse 3

            C
Well, come on, pretty baby, won't ya walk with me?

Come on, pretty baby, won't ya talk with me?

Come on, pretty baby, give me one more chance,

N.C.
  Try and save our romance.

          F
Slow down,

                      C
Baby, now you're movin' way too fast.

        G   F
You gotta gimme little lovin', gimme little lovin',

C N.C.   C
  Ow, if you want our love to last.

Something

Words and Music by
George Harrison

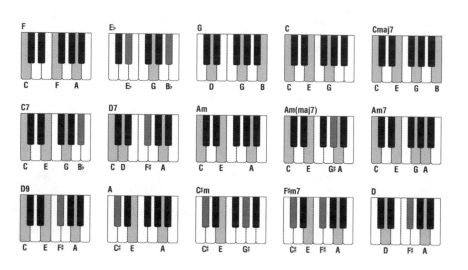

Intro

| F   Eb G/D |

Verse 1

    C   Cmaj7
Something in the way she moves

C7   F   F/E
  Attracts me like no other lover.

D7   G
Something in the way she woos me.

  Am   Am(maj7)
I don't want to leave her now,

   Am7   D9 F Eb G/D
You know I believe, and how.

Verse 2

  C   Cmaj7
  Somewhere in her smile she knows

  C7   F F/E
   That I don't need no other lover.

  D7   G
  Something in her style that shows me.

   Am   Am(maj7)
  I don't want to leave her now,

    Am7   D9
  You know I believe, and how.

  | F Eb G/D | A |

Bridge

  A   C#m/G#   F#m7 A/E
   You're asking me will my love grow,

    D   G   A
  I don't know, I don't know.

       C#m/G#   F#m7 A/E
   You stick a-round now, it may show,

    D   G   C
  I don't know, I don't know.

Solo

  | C | Cmaj7 | C7 | F F/E | D7 | G |
  | Am Am(maj7) | Am7 D9 | F Eb G/D |

Verse 3

  C   Cmaj7
  Something in the way she knows,

  C7   F   F/E
  And all I have to do is think of her.

  D7   G
  Something in the things she shows me.

   Am   Am(maj7)
  I don't want to leave her now,

    Am7   D9
  You know I believe, and how.

Outro

  | F Eb G/D | A | F Eb G/D | C

Sun King

Words and Music by John Lennon
and Paul McCartney

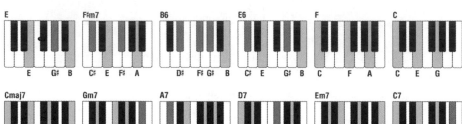

Intro

| E | | | | |

||: F#m7 | B6 | E6 | E :|| *Play 3 times*

F/G
Ah.

Chorus

C   Cmaj7   Gm7 A7
Here comes the Sun King.

C   Cmaj7   Gm7 A7
Here comes the Sun King.

F   D7
 Everybody's laugh-ing,

F   D7
 Everybody's hap-py.

C   Em7   C7 F
Here comes the Sun King.

Verse

F#m7   B6 E6 E
Quando paramucho mi amore defelice cara-fon.

F#m7   B6 E6 E
Mundo paparazzi mi amore chicka ferdy para-sol.

F#m7   B6 E6
Cuesto obrigado tanta mucho que can eat it carou-sel.

Taxman

Words and Music by
George Harrison

Let me ____ tell you ___ how it _____ will ___ be: ___

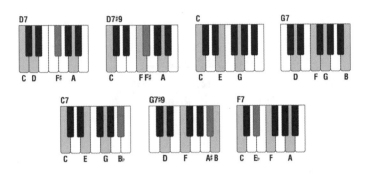

Intro | D7 | |

Verse 1

           D7   **D7♯9**
Let me tell you how it will be:

D7   **D7♯9**
  There's one for you, nineteen for me.

D7   **C**
'Cause I'm the Taxman.

               G7   **D7**
Yeah, I'm the ___ Taxman.

Verse 2

          D7   **D7$\sharp$9**
Should five percent appear too small,

D7   **D7$\sharp$9**
  Be thankful I don't take it all.

D7   **C**
  'Cause I'm the Taxman.

                G7   **D7**
Yeah, I'm the __ Taxman.

Bridge

          D7
(If you drive a car, car.) I'll tax the street.

                     C7
(If you try to sit, sit.) I'll tax your seat.

          D7
(If you get too cold, cold.) I'll tax the heat.

                     C7
(If you take a walk, walk.) I'll tax your feet…

D7
Taxman!

Solo

| **D7** | **D7$\sharp$9 D7** | | | | | **D7$\sharp$9 D7** |

          C
'Cause I'm the Taxman.

                G7$\sharp$9   **D7**
Yeah, I'm the __ Taxman.

Verse 3

                    D7
Don't ask me what I want it for.

D7#9   **D7**
(Ah, ah, Mis-ter Wilson!)

If you don't want to pay some more.

D7#9   **D7**
(Ah, ah, Mis-ter Heath!)

             C
'Cause I'm the Taxman.

            G7#9   **D7**
Yeah, I'm the __ Taxman.

Verse 4

                   D7
Now my advice for those who die,

D7#9   **D7**
(Taxman!)

Declare the pennies on your eyes.

D7#9   **D7**
(Taxman!)

             C
'Cause I'm the Taxman.

            G7#9   **D7**
Yeah, I'm the __ Taxman.

           F7
And you're working for no one but me.

Outro

| D7 | | | D7#9 D7 |
(Taxman!)

| | | | | D7#9 | | *Fade out*

Tell Me What You See

Words and Music by John Lennon
and Paul McCartney

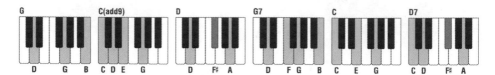

If you   let __ me __ your   heart, __

G   C(add9)   D   G7   C   D7

D G B   C D E   G   D   F♯ A   D F G B   C E G   C D   F♯ A

Intro |G | |

Verse 1
G   C(add9) D   G
If you let me   take your heart,

    C(add9) G
I will prove to you,

    C(add9) D   G
We will never   be a-part

C(add9) D   G
If   I'm   part of you.

Chorus 1
C(add9)   G   C(add9)   G
Open up your eyes now, tell me what you see.

C(add9)   G   C(add9) D   G
It is no sur-prise now, what you see is me.

Verse 2
G   C(add9) D   G
Big and black the clouds may be,

    C(add9) G
Time will pass a-way.

    C(add9) D   G
If you put your trust in me,

C(add9) D   G
I'll make bright your day.

Chorus 2

C(add9)   G   C(add9)   G
Look into these eyes now, tell me what you see.

C(add9)   G   C(add9) D   G
Don't you real-ize now, what you see is me?

Bridge 1

G7   C
Tell me what you see.

| G | | D7 | | G | | | | |

Verse 3

G   C(add9) D   G
Listen to   me   one more time,

          C(add9) G
How can I get   through?

            C(add9) D   G
Can't you try   to   see that I'm

C(add9) D   G
Trying to get to you?

Chorus 3

Repeat Chorus 1

Bridge 2

Repeat Bridge 1

Verse 4

G   C(add9) D   G
Listen to   me   one more time,

          C(add9) G
How can I get   through?

          C(add9) D   G
Can't you try   to   see that I'm

C(add9) D   G
Trying to get to you?

Chorus 4

C(add9)   G   C(add9)   G
Open up your eyes now, tell me what you see.

C(add9) G   C(add9) D   G
It is no sur-prise now, what you see is me.

G7   C   G
Mm, mm, mm, mm, mm.

Tell Me Why

Words and Music by John Lennon
and Paul McCartney

Melody:

Tell _ me   why _____ you cried, _

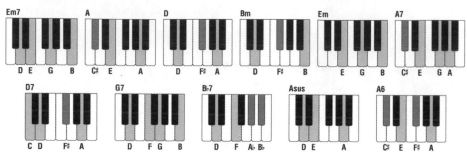

Intro
| Em7 A |Em7 A |Em7 A |

Chorus 1

Em7 A   D
    Tell me why you cried,

Em7   A   D Em7
    And why you lied to me.

A   D
Tell me why you cried,

Em7   A   D Em7   A
    And why you lied to me.

Verse 1

    D   Bm
Well, I gave you everything I had,

    Em   A7
But you left me sitting on my own,

    D   Bm
Did you have to treat me, oh, so bad?

    Em   A7
All I do is hang my head and moan.

Chorus 2

A   D
Tell me why you cried,

Em7   A   D Em7
    And why you lied to me.

A   D
Tell me why you cried,

Em7   A   D Em7   A
    And why you lied to me.

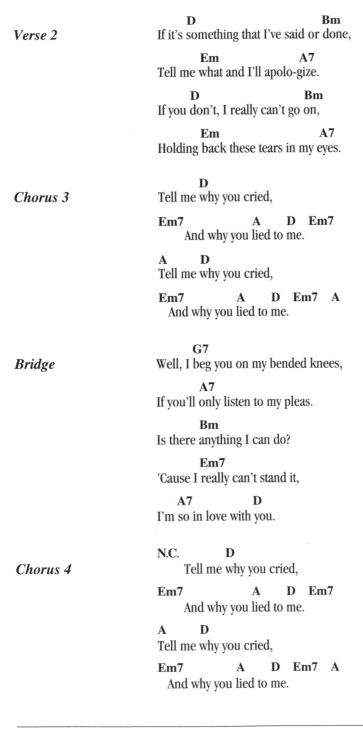

Verse 2

       D   **Bm**
If it's something that I've said or done,

       Em   **A7**
Tell me what and I'll apolo-gize.

       D   **Bm**
If you don't, I really can't go on,

       Em   **A7**
Holding back these tears in my eyes.

Chorus 3

         D
Tell me why you cried,

Em7   **A**   **D** **Em7**
  And why you lied to me.

A   **D**
Tell me why you cried,

Em7   **A**   **D** **Em7** **A**
  And why you lied to me.

Bridge

        G7
Well, I beg you on my bended knees,

       A7
If you'll only listen to my pleas.

       Bm
Is there anything I can do?

       Em7
'Cause I really can't stand it,

      A7   **D**
I'm so in love with you.

Chorus 4

N.C.   **D**
  Tell me why you cried,

Em7   **A**   **D** **Em7**
  And why you lied to me.

A   **D**
Tell me why you cried,

Em7   **A**   **D** **Em7** **A**
  And why you lied to me.

Thank You Girl

Words and Music by John Lennon
and Paul McCartney

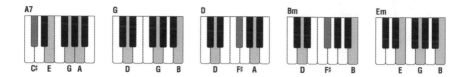

A7	G	D	Bm	Em
C# E G A	D G B	D F# A	D F# B	E G B

Intro

    |A7 |G |

Verse 1

    A7 G
    Oh, oh.

    D   G   D G
    You've ____ been good to me.

                D   A7   D   G
    You made me glad ____ when I was blue.

    D   G   D G
    And ____ eternal-ly,

              D   A7   D
    I'll always be ____ in love with you.

Chorus 1

            G   A7 G
    And all I gotta do is thank you girl,

    A7
    Thank you girl.

Verse 2

```
D  G              D    G
I ____ could tell the world

          D    A7        D    G
A thing or two ____ about our love.

D  G           D    G
I ____ know little girl,

       D    A7             D
Only a fool ____ would doubt our love.
```

Chorus 2   *Repeat Chorus 1*

Bridge

```
Bm           D          A7
Thank you girl for loving me the way that you do,

(Way that you do.)

Em            A7          D
That's the kind of love that is too good to be true.
```

Chorus 3

```
       G      A7  G
And all I gotta do is thank you girl,

A7             G
Thank you girl.
```

Verse 3   *Repeat Verse 1*

Chorus 4   *Repeat Chorus 3*

Outro

```
A7 G  D  G  D  G
Oh,  oh,  oh!

A7 G  D  G  D  G
Oh,  oh,  oh!

A7 G   D
Oh,  oh!
```

That Means a Lot

Words and Music by John Lennon
and Paul McCartney

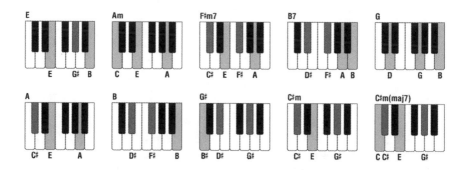

Intro | E | |

Verse 1

        E   Am   E
A friend says that your love won't mean a lot,

                        Am   F#m7 B7
But you know that your love is all you've got.

        G   Am   G   F#m7 B7
At times, things are so fine, and at times they're not.

        E   A
But when she says she loves you,

   B   E
That means a lot.

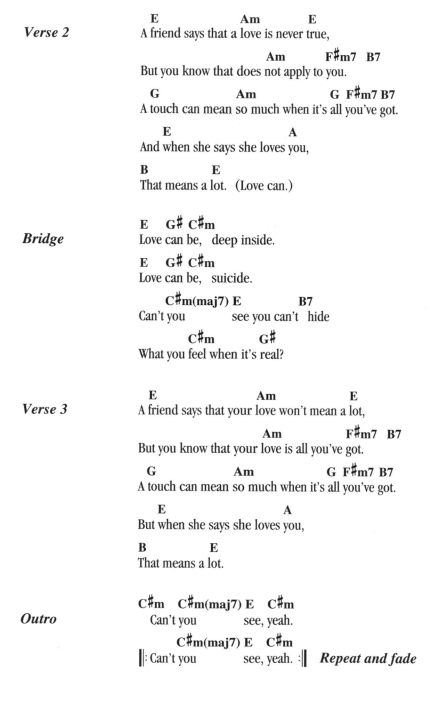

Verse 2

      E   Am   E
A friend says that a love is never true,

                      Am   F#m7 B7
But you know that does not apply to you.

    G   Am   G F#m7 B7
A touch can mean so much when it's all you've got.

      E   A
And when she says she loves you,

    B   E
That means a lot. (Love can.)

Bridge

      E   G# C#m
Love can be, deep inside.

      E   G# C#m
Love can be, suicide.

      C#m(maj7) E   B7
Can't you   see you can't hide

        C#m   G#
What you feel when it's real?

Verse 3

      E   Am   E
A friend says that your love won't mean a lot,

                 Am   F#m7 B7
But you know that your love is all you've got.

    G   Am   G F#m7 B7
A touch can mean so much when it's all you've got.

      E   A
But when she says she loves you,

    B   E
That means a lot.

Outro

    C#m   C#m(maj7) E   C#m
    Can't you   see, yeah.

        C#m(maj7) E   C#m
‖: Can't you   see, yeah. :‖ *Repeat and fade*

There's a Place

Words and Music by John Lennon
and Paul McCartney

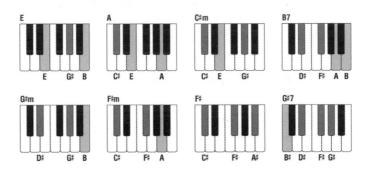

Intro | E | A | E | A |

Verse 1

    N.C.
There

      E   A   E
Is a place where I can go,

  A   E
When I feel low,

C#m   B7
When I feel blue,

       G#m A
And it's my mind,

         E   A
And there's no time

      F#m C#m/G
When I'm a-lone.

Verse 2

N.C.
I

       E
Think of you

A   E
And things you do

A   E
Go 'round my head,

C#m   B7
The things you've said,

       A   B7
Like, I love only you.

Bridge

C#m   F#
In my mind there's no sorrow,

E   G#7
Don't you know that it's so?

C#m   F#
There'll be no sad to-morrow,

E   G#7   C#m
Don't you know that it's so?

Verse 3

Repeat Verse 1

Outro

N.C.   E   A
There's a place.

         E   A
There's a place.

         E   A
There's a place.

           E   A
||: There's a place.   :|| *Repeat and fade*

Things We Said Today

Words and Music by John Lennon
and Paul McCartney

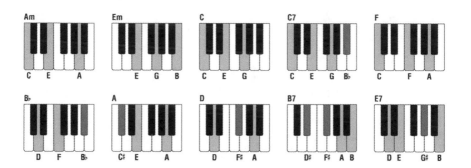

Intro | Am | | |

Verse 1

      Am   Em   Am   Em   Am
You say you will love me if I have to go.

           Em   Am   Em Am
You'll be thinking of me, somehow I will know.

C   C7
Someday when I'm lonely,

F   Bb
Wishing you weren't so far away.

Am   Em   Am   Em   Am
Then I will re-member things we said to-day.

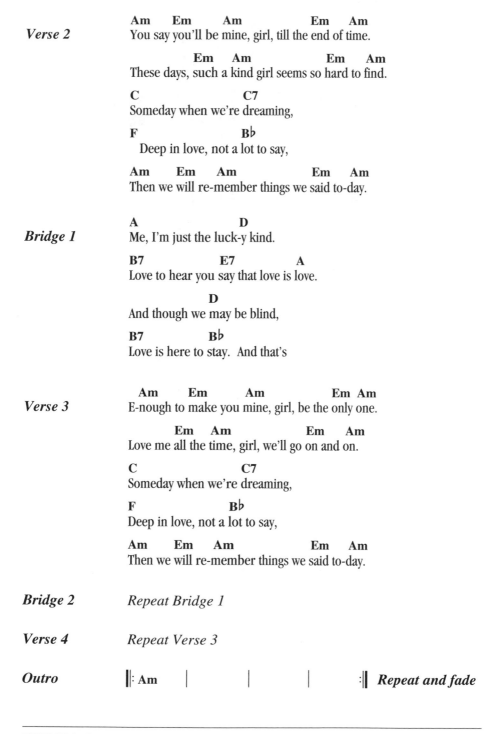

                    Am   Em   Am   Em   Am
Verse 2   You say you'll be mine, girl, till the end of time.

                            Em   Am   Em   Am
                    These days, such a kind girl seems so hard to find.

                    C   C7
                    Someday when we're dreaming,

                    F   B♭
                      Deep in love, not a lot to say,

                    Am   Em   Am   Em   Am
                    Then we will re-member things we said to-day.

                        A   D
Bridge 1   Me, I'm just the luck-y kind.

                    B7   E7   A
                    Love to hear you say that love is love.

                                    D
                    And though we may be blind,

                    B7   B♭
                    Love is here to stay. And that's

                        Am   Em   Am   Em Am
Verse 3   E-nough to make you mine, girl, be the only one.

                            Em   Am   Em   Am
                    Love me all the time, girl, we'll go on and on.

                    C   C7
                    Someday when we're dreaming,

                    F   B♭
                    Deep in love, not a lot to say,

                    Am   Em   Am   Em   Am
                    Then we will re-member things we said to-day.

Bridge 2   *Repeat Bridge 1*

Verse 4   *Repeat Verse 3*

Outro   ‖: Am | | | :‖ *Repeat and fade*

Think for Yourself

Words and Music by
George Harrison

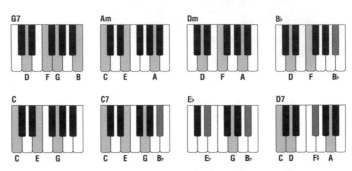

Intro

| G7 | | |

Verse 1

Am **Dm**
I've got a word or two

B♭   **C**   **G7**
To say a-bout the things that you do.

Am   **Dm**
You're telling all those lies

B♭   **C**   **G7**
About the good things that we can have

           Am
If we close our eyes.

Chorus 1

C7
Do what you want to do,

       G7
And go where you're going to.

E♭/B♭
Think for yourself,

       D7   **G7**
'Cause I won't be there with you.

Verse 2

Am   Dm
I left you far behind

B♭   C   G7
The ruins of the life that you have in mind.

Am   Dm
And though you still can't see,

B♭   C
I know your mind's made up.

      G7   Am
You're gonna cause more misery.

Chorus 2

Repeat Chorus 1

Verse 3

Am   Dm
Although your mind's opaque,

B♭   C
Try thinking more.

      G7
If just for your own sake.

Am   Dm
The future still looks good,

B♭   C   G7
And you've got time to recti-fy

      Am
All the things that you should.

Chorus 3

Repeat Chorus 1

Chorus 4

C7
Do what you want to do,

      G7
And go where you're going to.

E♭/B♭
Think for yourself,

      D7   C7 G7
'Cause I won't be there with you.

E♭/B♭
Think for yourself,

      D7   C7 G7
'Cause I won't be there with you.

This Boy
(Ringo's Theme)

Words and Music by John Lennon
and Paul McCartney

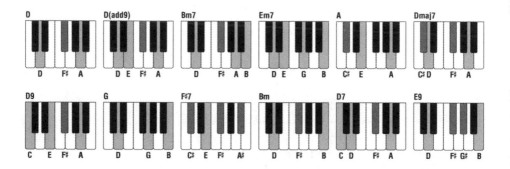

Intro |D   D(add9) D |D   Bm7 |Em7   A |

Verse 1

Dmaj7   Bm   Em7
That boy

         A   Dmaj7   Bm7
Took my love a-way,

Em7   A   Dmaj7   Bm7
   Though he'll re-gret it some-day.

      Em7 N.C.
But this   boy

A   N.C.   D   Bm7   Em7   A
Wants you back a-gain.

Verse 2

Dmaj7 Bm Em7
That boy

   A   Dmaj7 Bm7
Isn't good for you,

Em7   A   Dmaj7 Bm7
  Though he may want you too.

Em7 N.C.
This   boy

A   N.C.   D   D9
Wants you back a-gain.

Bridge

       G   F#7
Oh, and this boy would be happy,

      Bm   D   D7
Just to love you, but oh my-hi-hi-hi-a,

G   E9
That boy won't be happy

A   N.C.
Till he's seen you cry.

Verse 3

Dmaj7 Bm Em7
This boy

   A   Dmaj7 Bm7
Wouldn't mind the pain,

Em7   A   Dmaj7 Bm7
  Would always feel the same.

  Em7 N.C.
If this   boy

A   N.C.   D   Bm7 Em7 A
Gets you back a-gain.

Outro

Dmaj7 Bm Em7 A
This boy.

Dmaj7   Bm7 Em7 A
‖: This boy.   :‖ *Repeat and fade*

Ticket to Ride

Words and Music by John Lennon
and Paul McCartney

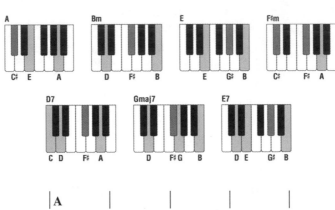

Intro | A | | | | |

Verse 1

    A
I think I'm gonna be sad, I think it's today, yeah.

    Bm   E
The girl that's driving me mad is going a-way.

F♯m   **D7**
She's got a ticket to ride.

F♯m   **Gmaj7**
She's got a ticket to ride.

F♯m   **E**   **A**
She's got a ticket to ride, and she don't care.

Verse 2

    A
She said that living with me was bringing her down, yeah.

    Bm   E
She would never be free when I was a-round.

F♯m   **D7**
She's got a ticket to ride.

F♯m   **Gmaj7**
She's got a ticket to ride.

F♯m   **E**   **A**
She's got a ticket to ride, and she don't care.

Bridge 1

        D7
I don't know why she's riding so high.

She ought to think twice,

            E   **E7**
She ought to do right by me.

    D7
Be-fore she gets to saying goodbye,

She ought to think twice,

            E
She ought to do right by me.

Verse 3

    A
I think I'm gonna be sad, I think it's today, yeah.

           Bm **E**
The girl that's driving me mad is going a-way, yeah!

   F#m   **D7**
Ah, she's got a ticket to ride.

F#m   **Gmaj7**
She's got a ticket to ride.

F#m   **E**   **A**
She's got a ticket to ride, and she don't care.

Bridge 2

Repeat Bridge 1

Verse 4

    A
She said that living with me was bringing her down, yeah.

        Bm **E**
She would never be free when I was a-round.

F#m   **D7**
She's got a ticket to ride.

F#m   **Gmaj7**
She's got a ticket to ride.

F#m   **E**   **A**
She's got a ticket to ride, and she don't care.

‖: My baby don't care. :‖   *Repeat and fade*

Tomorrow Never Knows

Words and Music by John Lennon
and Paul McCartney

Turn off your mind, re - lax and float down - stream. _

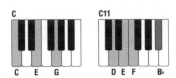

Intro |C | | | |

Verse 1

C
Turn off your mind,

Relax and float downstream.

C11   C
It is not dying, it is not dying.

Verse 2

C
Lay down all thought,

Surrender to the void.

C11   C
It is shining, it is shining.

Verse 3

C
That you may see

The meaning of within.

C11   C
It is being, it is being.

Solo   ‖: C | | | :‖

Verse 4
C
That love is all

And love is everyone.
C11   C
It is knowing, it is knowing.

Verse 5
C
That ignorance and hate

May mourn the dead.
C11   C
It is be-lieving, it is be-lieving.

Verse 6
C
But listen to the

Color of your dreams.
C11   C
It is not living, it is not living.

Verse 7
C
Or play the game existence to the end.
C11   C
Of the be-ginning, of the be-ginning.
C11   C
Of the be-ginning, of the be-ginning.
C11   C
Of the be-ginning, of the be-ginning.
C11   C
Of the be-ginning.

Twist and Shout

Words and Music by Bert Russell
and Phil Medley

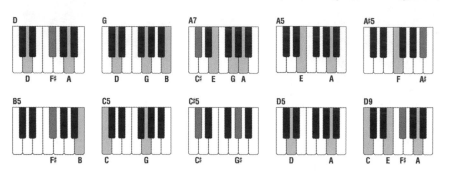

Intro | D G A7 | | D G A7 | |

                                   D
Chorus 1   Well, shake it up ba - by, now,

                 G   A7
                 (Shake it up, baby.)

                 D
                 Twist and shout.

                 G   A7
                 (Twist and shout.)

                                              D
                 Come on, come on, come on, come on, baby now.

                 G   A7
                 (Come on, baby.)

                             D
                 Come on and work it on out.

                 G   A7
                 (Work it on out.)

	D
Verse 1	Well, work it on out.

G   **A7**
(Work it on out.)

                             D
You know you look so good.

G   **A7**
(Look so good.)

                     D
You know you got me goin' now.

G   **A7**
(Got me goin'.)

                      D
Just like I knew you would.

       G   **A7**
(Like I knew you would. Oo.)

Chorus 2   **Repeat Chorus 1**

	D
Verse 2	You know you twist, little girl.

G   **A7**
(Twist little girl.)

                   D
You know you twist so fine.

G   **A7**
(Twist so fine.)

                        D
Come on and twist a little closer now,

G   **A7**
(Twist a little closer.)

                      D
And let me know that you're mine.

       G   **A7**
(Let me know you're mine, ooh.)

Interlude ‖: D G A7 | G A7 :‖ *Play 4 times*

Ah, ah, ah, ah. Wow!

Chorus 3 **Repeat Chorus 1**

Verse 3 **Repeat Verse 2**

                                    D
Outro Well, shake it, shake it, shake it, baby, now.

        G   **A7**
        (Shake it up, baby.)

                                    D
        Well, shake it, shake it, shake, it, baby, now.

        G   **A7**
        (Shake it up, baby. Oo.)

                A5 A♯5 B5 C5 C♯5 D5 N.C. D9
        Ah, ah, ah, ah.

What's the New Mary Jane

Words and Music by John Lennon
and Paul McCartney

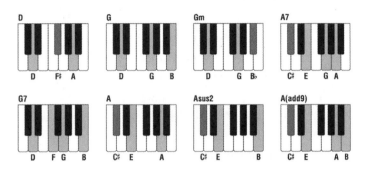

Intro　　　　　|D G/B Gm/B♭|A7　|D G/B Gm/B♭|A7　　|

　　　　　　　　　　　D　　　　　G/B Gm/B♭ A7
Verse 1　　　She looks as an Afri - can　　queen.

　　　　　　　　　　　D　　　　　　　G/B Gm/B♭ A7
　　　　　　　　She eating twelve cha-pattis and　　cream.

　　　　　　　　　　　D　　　　　G/B Gm/B♭ A7
　　　　　　　　She taste as Mon - go - lian　　lamb.

　　　　　　　　　　　D　　　　　G/B Gm/B♭ A7
　　　　　　　　She coming from Alde - be　-　ran.

　　　　　　　　G7/A　　　　　　　　　　　　　　　　　　A　　Asus2 A
Chorus 1　　　What a shame Mary Jane had a pain at the party.

　　　　　　　　G7/A
　　　　　　　　What a shame Mary Jane,

　　　　　　　　　　　　　　　　　　　　　　　　　　A　　Asus2 A
　　　　　　　　What a shame Mary Jane had a pain at the party.

Verse 2

        D   G/B   Gm/B♭ A7
She like to be married with   Yeti.

        D   G/B   Gm/B♭ A7
He grooving such cookie spa - ghetti.

        D   G/B Gm/B♭ A7
She jumping as Mexi - can   bean,

        D   G/B Gm/B♭ A7
To make that her body more   thin.

Chorus 2   *Repeat Chorus 1*

        D   G/B   Gm/B♭ A7
Verse 3   She catch Pata-gonian pan - cakes,

        D   G/B   Gm/B♭ A7
With that one and gin par-ty   makes.

        D   G/B Gm/B♭ A7
She having al-ways good   contacts,

        D   G/B Gm/B♭ A7
She making with apple and   contract.

G7/A   A   Asus2 A
Chorus 3   What a shame Mary Jane had a pain at the party.

G7/A
   What a shame Mary Jane,

                               A   Asus2 A
What a shame Mary Jane had a pain at the party.

(All together now!)

Chorus 4	**G7/A** **A** **Asus2** **A** What a shame Mary Jane had a pain at the party.

G7/A
What a shame,

                                       A   **Asus2**   **A**
What a shame Mary Jane had a pain at the party.

G7/A
What a shame, what a shame,

                                       A
What a shame Mary Jane had a pain at the party.

G7/A
What a shame, what a shame, what a shame,

                                       A
What a shame Mary Jane had a pain at the party…

Interlude	‖: **A** **A(add9) A** **A(add9)** │ **A** **A(add9) A** **A(add9)** :‖

       D   **G/B** **Gm/B♭ A7**
She looks as an Afri - can   queen.

       D   **G/B** **Gm/B♭ A7**
She taste as Mon - go - lian   lamb.

G7/A
What a shame Mary Jane,

                                       A   **Asus2**   **A**
What a shame Mary Jane had a pain at the party.

(All together now!)

Chorus 5	***Repeat Chorus 3 till fade***

Two of Us

Words and Music by John Lennon
and Paul McCartney

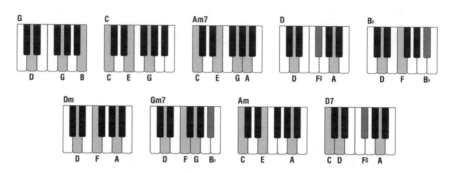

Intro | G | | | | | |

Verse 1

G
Two of us riding nowhere,

                        C   G/B   Am7
Spending someone's hard-earned pay.

G
You and me Sunday driving,

                    C G/B Am7   G
Not arriving on our   way back home.

Chorus 1

D   C G
We're on our way home.

D   C G
We're on our way home.

C   G
We're going home.

Verse 2

G
Two of us sending postcards,

          C G/B Am7
Writing letters on my   wall.

G
You and me burning matches,

          C G/B Am7   G
Lifting latches, on our   way back home.

Chorus 2   *Repeat Chorus 1*

Bridge 1

B♭   Dm
You and I have memories,

Gm7   Am   D7
Longer than the road that stretches out ahead.

Verse 3

G
Two of us wearing raincoats,

          C G/B Am7
Standing solo in the   sun.

G
You and me chasing paper,

          C G/B Am7   G
Getting nowhere on our   way back home.

Chorus 3   *Repeat Chorus 1*

Bridge 2   *Repeat Bridge 1*

Verse 4   *Repeat Verse 3*

Chorus 4   *Repeat Chorus 1*

Outro |G | ‖: | | | :‖ *Repeat and fade*

Wait

Words and Music by John Lennon
and Paul McCartney

Melody:

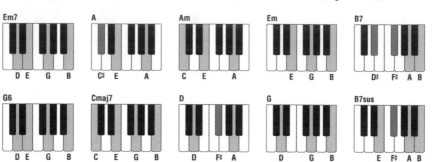

It's been a   long   time, —

Verse 1

             Em7 A/E
It's been a long time,

Am/E Em B7   **Em**
Now   I'm coming back home.

            Em7 A/E
I've been a-way now,

Am/E Em B7   **Em**
Oh,   how I've been a-lone.

Chorus 1

G6   Cmaj7 G6   **Cmaj7 G6 Cmaj7**
Wait   till I come back to your side,

        G6   **B7**   **Em**
We'll for-get the tears we cried.

Verse 2

           Em7 A/E
But if your heart breaks,

Am/E Em B7   **Em**
Don't wait, turn me a-way.

          Em7   A/E
And if your heart's strong,

Am/E Em B7   **Em**
Hold   on, I won't de-lay.

Chorus 2	*Repeat Chorus 1*

Bridge 1

          A   **D**
I feel as though you ought to know

           G   **Em**
That I've been good, as good as I can be.

         A   **D**
And if you do, I'll trust in you,

          G   **B7sus** **B7**
And know that you will wait for me.

Verse 3	*Repeat Verse 1*
Chorus 3	*Repeat Chorus 1*
Bridge 2	*Repeat Bridge 1*
Verse 4	*Repeat Verse 2*
Chorus 4	*Repeat Chorus 1*

Verse 5

      Em7 A/E
It's been a long time,

Am/E Em B7   **Em**
Now   I'm coming back home.

      Em7 A/E
I've been a-way now,

Am/E Em B7   **Em**
Oh,   how I've been alone.

We Can Work It Out

Words and Music by John Lennon
and Paul McCartney

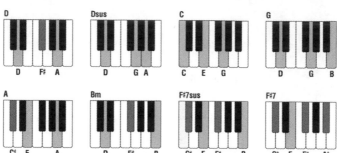

Verse 1

    D   **Dsus D**
    Try to see it my   way.

                Dsus   **C**   **D**
Do I have to keep on talking till I can't go on?

               Dsus D
While you see it your   way,

                Dsus   **C**   **D**
Run the risk of knowing that our love may soon be gone.

Chorus 1

G   **D**
We can work it out.

G   **A**
We can work it out.

Verse 2

    D   **Dsus D**
    Think of what you're say - ing.

                Dsus   **C**   **D**
You can get it wrong and still you think that it's al-right.

                Dsus D
Think of what I'm say - ing.

                Dsus   **C**   **D**
We can work it out and get it straight, or say good-night.

Chorus 2   *Repeat Chorus 1*

Bridge 1

Bm   Bm/A   G   F#7sus
Life is very short, and there's no time

   F#7   Bm   Bm/A Bm/G Bm/F#
For fussing and fighting, my friend.

Bm   Bm/A G   F#7sus
I have always thought that it's a crime,

   F#7 Bm   Bm/A Bm/G Bm/F#
So I will ask you once a - gain.

Verse 3

D   Dsus D
 Try to see it my   way.

        Dsus   C   D
Only time will tell if I am right or I am wrong.

        Dsus D
While you see it your   way,

         Dsus   C   D
There's a chance that we might fall a-part before too long.

Chorus 3   *Repeat Chorus 1*

Bridge 2   *Repeat Bridge 1*

Verse 4   *Repeat Verse 3*

Chorus 4

G   D
We can work it out.

G   A   D
We can work it out.

What Goes On

Words and Music by John Lennon,
Paul McCartney and Richard Starkey

Melody:

What goes on _____ in your heart?

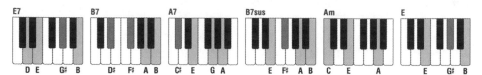

E7   B7   A7   B7sus   Am   E

D E G♯ B   D♯ F♯ A B   C♯ E G A   E F♯ A B   C E A   E G♯ B

Intro | E7 B7 | E7 |

Chorus 1
               E7
What goes on in your heart?

                  A7
What goes on in your mind?

         E7
You are tearing me apart,

                  A7
When you treat me so un-kind.

         B7sus B7   **E**
What goes on _____ in your mind?

Verse 1
         E7
The other day I saw you

         Am
As I walked along the road.

         E7
But when I saw him with you,

           Am
I could feel my future fold.

             B7   **E7**
It's so easy for a girl like you to lie.

         B7
Tell me why.

Chorus 2   *Repeat Chorus 1*

       E7

Verse 2   I met you in the morning,

         Am

       Waiting for the tides of time.

       E7

       But now the tide is turning,

         Am

       I can see that I was blind.

           B7   **E7**

       It's so easy for a girl like you to lie.

         B7

       Tell me why.

         E7

       What goes on in your heart?

Solo | **E7** | **A7** | **E7** | |

       | | **A7** | **B7** | **E7** |

       E7

Verse 3   I used to think of no one else,

         Am

       But you were just the same.

         E7

       You didn't even think of me

         Am

       As someone with a name.

              B7   **E7**

       Did you mean to break my heart and watch me die?

         B7

       Tell me why.

Chorus 3   *Repeat Chorus 1*

Outro | **E7** | | **E**

What You're Doing

Words and Music by John Lennon
and Paul McCartney

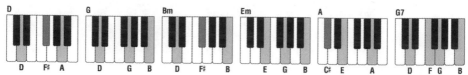

Intro | *Drums for 4 bars* |D |G |D |G |

Verse 1

D   G
Look what you're doing,

D   G
I'm feeling blue and lonely.

     Bm   G
Would it be too much to ask of you,

                D   G
What you're doing to me?

Verse 2

D   G
You got me running

D   G
And there's no fun in it.

     Bm   G
Why should it be so much to ask of you,

             D
What you're doing to me?

Bridge 1

G   Bm
 I've been waiting here for you,

G   Bm
 Wondering what you're gonna do.

Em
 And should you need a love that's true,

   A
It's me.

Verse 3

D   G
Please stop your lying,

D   G
You've got me crying, girl.

                Bm   G
Why should it be so much to ask of you,

                        D   G
What you're doing to me?

Solo

| D | G7 | D | G7 | |
| Bm | G7 | | D | |

Bridge 2

Repeat Bridge 1

Verse 4

D   G
Please stop your lying,

D   G
You've got me crying, girl.

                Bm   G
Why should it be so much to ask of you,

                      D
What you're doing to me?

                G   D
What you're doing to me?

                G   D G
What you're doing to me?

| D | *Drums* | A | | |

Outro

‖: D | G7 | D | G7 :‖   *Repeat and fade*

When I Get Home

Words and Music by John Lennon
and Paul McCartney

Melody:

Whoa, _____ I, _____

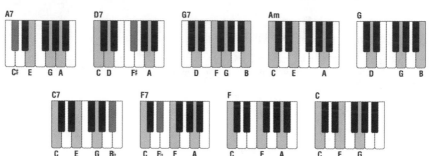

A7   C# E   G A
D7   C D   F# A
G7   D   F G   B
Am   C   E   A
G   D   G   B

C7   C E G Bb
F7   C Eb F A
F   C   F A
C   C E G

Chorus 1

       A7
Whoa, I, whoa, I,

      D7   **G7**
I got a whole lot of things to tell her

           Am   **G**
When I get home.

Verse 1

      C7   **F7**
Come on, out my way.

         C7   **F7**
'Cause I'm a gonna see my baby to-day.

       C7   **F7**   **G7**
I've got a whole lot of things I've gotta say to her.

Chorus 2

Repeat Chorus 1

Verse 2

      C7   **F7**
Come on if you please.

      C7   **F7**
I've got no time for triviali-ty.

      C7   **F7**   **G7**
I've got a girl who's waiting home for me to-night.

Chorus 3

      A7
Whoa, I, whoa, I,

      D7   **G7**
I got a whole lot of things to tell her

          Am   **G**
When I get home.

Bridge

          C7
When I'm getting home tonight,

       Am
I'm gonna hold her tight.

       C7   **Am**
I'm gonna love her till the cows come home.

     F   **G**
I bet I'll love her more

     F   **G**   **Am G**
Till I walk out that door, a-gain.

Verse 3

       C7   **F7**
Come on, let me through.

       C7   **F7**
I've got so many things I've got to do.

       C7   **F7**   **G7**
I've got no business being here with you this way.

Chorus 4

      A7
Whoa, I, whoa, I,

      D7   **G7**
I got a whole lot of things to tell her

       A7
When I get home, yeah.

      D7   **G7**
I got a whole lot of things to tell her

          C
When I get home.

When I'm Sixty-Four

Words and Music by John Lennon
and Paul McCartney

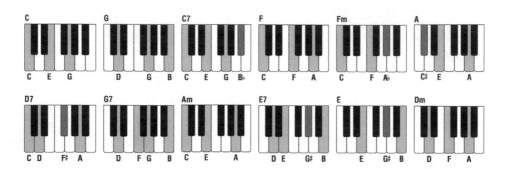

When I get old - er, los - ing my hair, —

Verse 1

    C
When I get older, losing my hair,

              G
Many years from now,

Will you still be sending me a valentine,

    N.C.   **C**
Birth-day greetings, bottle of wine?

If I'd been out 'til quarter to three,

C7   **F**
Would you lock the door?

            Fm
Will you still need__ me?

C   **A**
Will you still feed__ me,

D7   **G7** **C**
When I'm sixty-four?

Bridge 1

Am/E E7   Am G/B F/C G/B G Am
Ooh.

            E N.C. Am
You'll be older, too.

      Dm
And if you say the word,

F   G   C   G7
I could stay with you.

Verse 2

C
I could be handy mending a fuse

                    G7
When your lights have gone.

You can knit a sweater by the fireside.

    N.C.   C
Sun-day morning go for a ride.

Doing the garden, digging the weeds,

C7   F
Who could ask for more?

        Fm
Will you still need__ me?

C   A
Will you still feed__ me,

D7   G7 C
When I'm sixty-four?

Bridge 2

Am/E   E7   Am
Ev'ry summer we can rent a cottage

        G/B F/C   G/B   G   Am
In the Isle of Wight,__ if it's not too dear.

               E   N.C. Am
We shall scrimp and save.

        Dm
Grandchildren on your knee;

F   G   C   G7
Vera, Chuck, and Dave.

Verse 3

C
Send me a postcard, drop me a line,

                  G
Stating point of view.

Indicate precisely what you mean to say.

      N.C.   C
Yours sincerely wasting away.

Give me your answer, fill in a form,

C7   F
Mine forevermore.

          Fm
A will you still need__ me?

C   A
Will you still feed__ me,

D7   G7 C
When I'm sixty-four?

Why Don't We Do It in the Road

Words and Music by John Lennon
and Paul McCartney

Why don't we d'-do it in the road? _____

Verse 1

N.C.   **D7**
Why don't we do it in the road?

Why don't we do it in the road?
                               G7
Why don't we do it in the road?
                               D7
Why don't we do it in the road?
A7
No one will be watching us.
G7   **D7**
Why don't we do it in the road?

Verse 2   *Repeat Verse 1*

Verse 3

N.C.   **D7**
Why don't we do it in the road?

Why don't we do it in the road?
                               G7
Why don't we do it in the road?
                               D7
Why don't we do it in the road?
A7
No one will be watching us.
N.C.   **D7**
Why don't we do it in the road?

While My Guitar Gently Weeps

Words and Music by
George Harrison

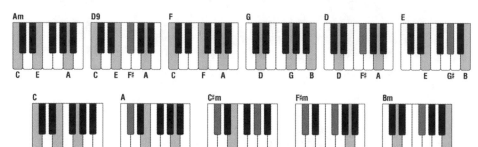

Intro

| Am | | Am/G | | D9/F# | | F | | |
| Am | | G | | D | | E | | |

Verse 1

    Am   Am/G   D9/F#   F
I look at you all, see the love there that's sleeping,

    Am   G   D   E
  While my gui-tar gently weeps.

    Am   Am/G   D9/F#   F
I look at the floor, and I see it needs sweeping.

    Am   G   C   E
  Still my gui-tar gently weeps.

Bridge 1

    A   C#m F#m   C#m
  I don't know why   nobody told you

    Bm   E
  How to unfold your love.

    A   C#m F#m   C#m
  I don't know how   someone con-trolled you.

    Bm   E
  They bought and sold you.

Verse 2

    Am   Am/G   D9/F#   F
I look at the world and I notice it's turning,

 Am   G   D   E
  While my gui-tar gently weeps.

       Am   Am/G   D9/F#   F
With every mis-take, we must surely be learning.

 Am   G   C   E
  Still my gui-tar gently weeps.

Solo

Am	Am/G	D9/F#	F
Am	G	D	E
Am	Am/G	D9/F#	F
Am	G	C	E

Bridge 2

 A   C#m F#m   C#m
  I don't know how   you were di-verted,

 Bm   E
  You were perverted too.

 A   C#m F#m   C#m
  I don't know how   you were in-verted.

 Bm   E
  No one alerted you.

Verse 3

    Am   Am/G   D9/F#   F
I look at you all, see the love there that's sleeping,

 Am   G   D E
  While my gui-tar gently weeps.

    Am   Am/G D9/F# F
I look at you all.

 Am   G   C   E
  Still my gui-tar gently weeps.

Outro

Am	Am/G	D9/F#	F
Am	G	D	E
Am	Am/G	D9/F#	F
Am	G	C	E
‖: Am	Am/G	D9/F#	F
Am	G	C	E :‖ *Repeat and fade*

Wild Honey Pie

Words and Music by John Lennon
and Paul McCartney

Melody:

Hon - ey pie. ___

G7	F7	E7	Eb7	D7
D F G B	C Eb F A	D E G# B	Db Eb G Bb	C D F# A

Intro | G7 | F7 | E7   Eb7 | D7 |

Verse 1
G7
Honey Pie.

Honey Pie.

Interlude 1 | G7 | F7 | E7   Eb7 | D7 |

Verse 2
G7
Honey Pie.

Honey Pie.

Interlude 2   *Repeat Interlude 1*

Verse 3
G7
Honey Pie.

F7
Honey Pie.

G7
Honey Pie.

F7
Honey Pie.

  G7
I love you, Honey Pie.

With a Little Help from My Friends

Words and Music by John Lennon
and Paul McCartney

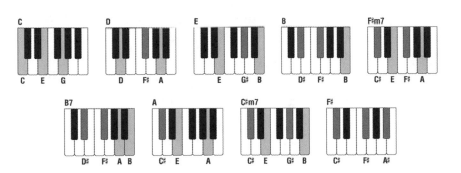

Intro

     C D E
Bil - ly Shears.

Verse 1

  E   **B**   **F♯m7**
What would you think if I sang out of tune,

          B7   **E**
Would you stand up and walk out on me?

     B   **F♯m7**
Lend me your ears and I'll sing you a song,

     B7   **E**
And I'll try not to sing out of key.

Chorus 1

     D   **A**   **E**
Oh, I get by with a little help from my friends.

     D   **A**   **E**
Mm, I get high with a little help from my friends.

        A   **E**   **B**
Mm, I'm gonna try with a little help from my friends.

Verse 2

E B   F#m7
What do I do when my love is away?

       B7 E
(Does it worry you to be a-lone?)

    B F#m7
How do I feel at the end of the day?

       B7 E
(Are you sad because you're on your own?)

Chorus 2

    D   A   E
No, I get by with a little help from my friends.

    D   A   E
Mm, I get high with a little help from my friends.

     A   E
Mm, gonna try with a little help from my friends.

Bridge 1

    C#m7 F#
(Do you need any-body?)

   E   D   A
I need some-body to love.

    C#m7 F#
(Could it be any-body?)

   E   D   A
I want some-body to love.

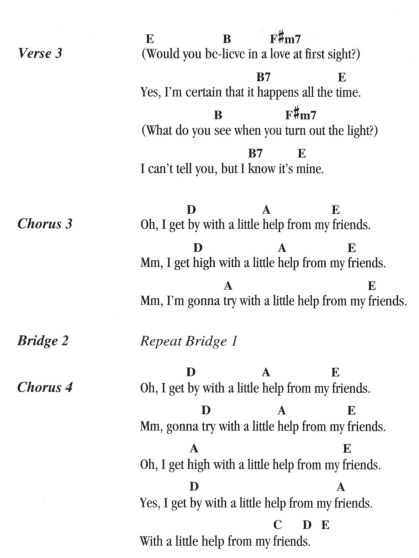

Verse 3

    E   B   F#m7
(Would you bc-licvc in a love at first sight?)

                 B7   E
Yes, I'm certain that it happens all the time.

          B   F#m7
(What do you see when you turn out the light?)

          B7   E
I can't tell you, but I know it's mine.

Chorus 3

         D   A   E
Oh, I get by with a little help from my friends.

         D   A   E
Mm, I get high with a little help from my friends.

      A   E
Mm, I'm gonna try with a little help from my friends.

Bridge 2   *Repeat Bridge 1*

Chorus 4

         D   A   E
Oh, I get by with a little help from my friends.

         D   A   E
Mm, gonna try with a little help from my friends.

      A   E
Oh, I get high with a little help from my friends.

         D   A
Yes, I get by with a little help from my friends.

                 C   D E
With a little help from my friends.

Within You Without You

Words and Music by
George Harrison

Melody:

We were talk - ing ____

C5   C   Csus   C7   Csus2

C   G   C E G   C   F G   C E G B♭   D E G

Intro ‖: C5 | | | | :‖ C | |

Verse 1

C Csus C5 C7
We were talk-ing

 C   Csus2 C   Csus C
About the space be - tween us   all,

       Csus C5 C7
And the   peo-ple

       C   Csus2 C Csus C   Csus C
Who hide themselves be - hind a   wall of illu - sion,

       Csus C
Nev-er   glimpse the truth.

          Csus C7 C   Csus   C
Then it's far too late, when they pass a-way.

Verse 2

C Csus C5 C7
We were talk-ing

 C   Csus2 C Csus C
A-bout the love we   all would share

       Csus C5 C7
When we   find it,

       C   Csus2 C   Csus C
To try our best to   hold it   there.

       Csus C   Csus   C7
With our   love, with our love

C Csus C   C7 C
We could save the world, if they only knew.

Bridge 1

C5
Try to realize it's all within yourself,

        C   Csus C
No one else can make you   change.

C5
And to see you're really only very small,

        C Csus C Csus2
And life flows on within you and with - out you.

Solo

‖: C5 | | | :‖ *Play 8 times*
| | | |

Verse 3

C Csus C5 C7
We were talk-ing

 C   Csus2 C   Csus C
About the love that's gone so   cold

     Csus C5 C7
And the   peo-ple

     C   Csus2 C   Csus C
Who gain the world and   lose their soul.

     Csus C
They don't know,

     Csus C
They can't see.

     Csus C   C7 C
Are you   one of   them?

Interlude

| C5 | | | | | | |

Bridge 2

C5
When you've seen beyond yourself,

                    C   Csus C
Then you may find peace of mind is wait-ing   there.

C5
And the time will come when you see we're all one.

               C Csus C Csus2
And life flows on within you and with - out you.

The Word

Words and Music by John Lennon
and Paul McCartney

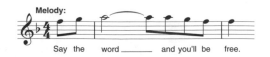

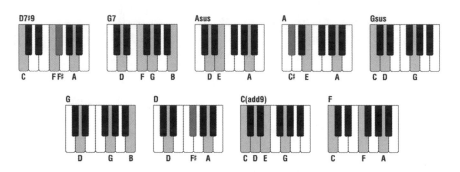

Intro |D7#9 | |

Chorus 1

D7#9
Say the word and you'll be free.

Say the word and be like me.

G7
Say the word I'm thinking of.

D7#9
Have you heard? The word is love.

Asus A ꞏ Gsus G
It's so   fine, it's sun - shine.

D7#9
It's the word love.

Verse 1

D   **C(add9)**
In the beginning, I misunderstood.

F   **G**
But now I've got it, the word is good.

		D7♯9
Chorus 2		Spread the word and you'll be free.

Spread the word and be like me.

G7
Spread the word I'm thinking of.

D7♯9
Have you heard? The word is love.

Asus A   **Gsus G**
It's so   fine, it's sun - shine.

D7♯9
It's the word love.

D   **C(add9)**

Verse 2   Everywhere I go I hear it said,

F   **G**
      In the good and the bad books that I have read.

Chorus 3   *Repeat Chorus 1*

D   **C(add9)**

Verse 3   Now that I know what I feel must be right,

F   **G**
      I'm here to show every-body the light.

Chorus 4

D7♯9
Give the word a chance to say,

That the word is just the way.

G7
It's the word I'm thinking of,

D7♯9
And the only word is love.

Asus A   Gsus G
It's so   fine, it's sun - shine.

D7♯9
It's the word love.

Solo |D |C(add9)|F |G |D7♯9 | |

D7♯9
Outro
Say the word love.

G7
Say the word love.

D7♯9
Say the word love.

Asus A Gsus G   D7♯9
Say the word _____ love.

|D |C(add9) |F *Fade out*

Yer Blues

Words and Music by John Lennon
and Paul McCartney

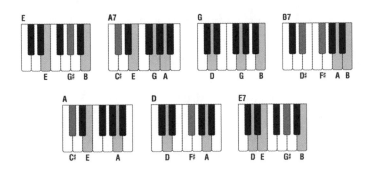

Verse 1

        E
Yes, I'm lonely, wanna die.

       A7   **E**
Yes, I'm lonely, wanna die.

      G
If I ain't   dead already,

B7   **E A E B7**
Whoo, girl, you know the reason why.

Verse 2

        E
In the morning, wanna die.

       A7   **E**
In the evening, wanna die.

      G
If I ain't   dead already,

B7   **E A E B7**
Whoo, girl, you know the reason why.

Bridge 1	E N.C.
	My moth-er was of the sky,
	
	D E N.C.
	  My fa-ther was of the earth.
	
	D E N.C.
	  But I am of the universe,
	
	   E7
	And you know what it's worth.

Verse 3	A7 E I'm lonely, wanna die. G If I ain't dead already, B7 E A E B7 Whoo, girl, you know the reason why.

Bridge 2	E N.C.
	The ea-gle picks my eyes.
	
	D E N.C.
	  The worm, he licks my bones.
	
	D E N.C.
	  Feel so suicidal,
	
	      E7
	Just like Dylan's Mr. Jones.

Verse 4	A7 E
	  Lonely, wanna die.
	
	      G
	If I ain't dead already,
	
	B7 E A E B7
	Whoo, girl, you know the reason why.

Verse 5

   E   N.C.
Black cloud crossed my mind,

   D E   N.C.
  Blue mist from my soul.

   D E   N.C.
  Feel so suicidal,

     E7
Even hate my rock and roll.

     A7   **E**
Wanna die, yeah, wanna die.

       G
If I ain't dead already,

B7   **E A E B7**
Whoo, girl, you know the reason why.

Solo

E			A7	
E		G	B7	E A	E B7
E			A7	
E		G	B7	E	

Verse 6

       E
(Yes, I'm lonely, wanna die.

      A7   **E**
Yes, I'm lonely, wanna die.

     G
If I ain't dead already,

B7   **E A E B7**
Girl, you know the reason why.)   ***Fade out***

Yellow Submarine

Words and Music by John Lennon
and Paul McCartney

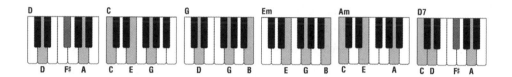

          D   C   G

Verse 1   In the town where I was born

              Em   Am   C   D
              Lived a man who sailed the sea.

              G   D   C   G
              And he told us of his life

              Em   Am   C   D
              In the land of subma-rines.

          D   C   G

Verse 2   So we sailed up to the sun

              Em   Am   C   D
              Till we found the sea of green.

              G   D   C   G
              And we lived be-neath the waves

              Em   Am   C   D
              In our yellow subma-rine.

                          G   D
Chorus 1   We all live in a yellow submarine,

                                      G
                Yellow submarine, yellow submarine.

                                  D
                We all live in a yellow submarine,

                                      G
                Yellow submarine, yellow submarine.

                              D   C   G
Verse 3   And our friends are all on board,

                Em   Am   C   D
                Many more of them live next door.

                G   D   C   G   D G   D7 G
                And the band be-gins to play.

Chorus 2   **Repeat Chorus 1**

                              D   C   G
Verse 4   As we live a life of ease,

                Em   Am   C   D
                Ev'ry one of us has all we need.

                G   D   C   G
                Sky of blue and sea of green

                Em   Am   C   D
                In our yellow subma-rine.

Chorus 3   **Repeat Chorus 1 till fade**

Yes It Is

Words and Music by John Lennon
and Paul McCartney

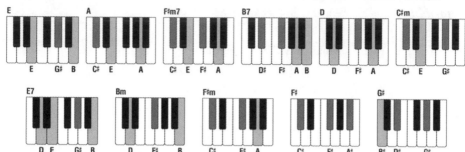

Intro | E |

Verse 1

E   A   F#m7 B7
If you wear red to-night,

    E   A   D   B7
Re-member what I said to-night.

    C#m/G#   A
For red is the color that my baby wore.

D   C#m
And what's more, it's true,

E
Yes it is.

Verse 2

E   A   F#m7 B7
Scarlet were the clothes she wore;

E   A   D   B7
Everybody knows I'm sure.

C#m/G#   A
I would remember all the things we planned.

D   C#m
Understand, it's true.

E   E7
Yes, it is, it's true. Yes, it is.

Bridge 1

Bm   E   A   F#m
I could be happy with you by my side,

Bm   E
If I could for-get her.

    C#m
But it's my pride,

       E
Yes it is, yes it is.

       F# B7
Oh, yes, it is,   yeah.

Verse 3

E   A   F#m7   B7
Please don't wear red to-night;

E   A   D   B7
This is what I said to-night.

   C#m/G#   A
For red is the color that will make me blue.

    D   C#m
In spite of you, it's true.

E
Yes it is, it's true.

E7
Yes it is.

Bridge 2   *Repeat Bridge 1*

Verse 4

E   A   F#m7   B7
Please don't wear red to-night;

E   A   D   B7
This is what I said to-night.

   C#m/G#   A
For red is the color that will make me blue.

    D   C#m
In spite of you, it's true.

E   G#
Yes it is, it's true.

A   E
Yes it is, it's true.

Yesterday

Words and Music by
John Lennon and
Paul McCartney

Yes-ter-day, _   all my trou-bles seemed so   far   a-way. _

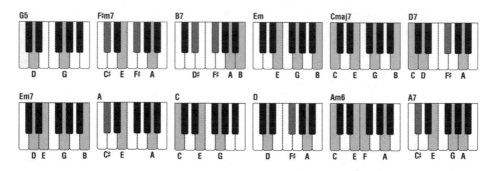

Intro |G5 | |

                                                                          G5   F#m7

Verse 1   Yesterday,

                           B7   Em   Em/D
All my troubles seemed so far away.

           Cmaj7 D7   G5   G5/F#
Now it looks as though they're here to stay.

           Em7   A   C   G5
Oh, I believe___ in yes - terday.

           G5   F#m7

Verse 2   Suddenly,

                       B7   Em   Em/D
I'm not half the man I used to be.

           Cmaj7   D7   G5   G5/F#
There's a shad - ow hanging over me,

           Em7   A   C   G5
Oh, yesterday___ came sud - denly.

Bridge 1

F#m7 B7 Em D C
Why she had to go

Em/B Am6 D7 G5
I don't know, she wouldn't say.

F#m7 B7 Em D C
I said some-thing wrong.

Em/B Am6 D7 G5
Now I___ long for yester-day.

Verse 3

G5 F#m7
Yesterday,

B7 Em Em/D
Love was such an easy game to play.

Cmaj7 D7 G5 G5/F#
Now I need a place to hide away.

Em7 A C G5
Oh, I believe___ in yes - terday.

Bridge 2

Repeat Bridge 1

Verse 4

G5 F#m7
Yesterday,

B7 Em Em/D
Love was such an easy game to play.

Cmaj7 D7 G5 G5/F#
Now I need a place to hide away.

Em7 A C G5
Oh, I believe___ in yes - terday.

G A7 C G5
Mm.

You Can't Do That

Words and Music by John Lennon
and Paul McCartney

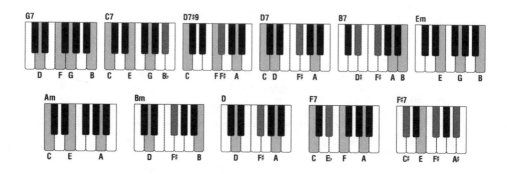

Intro | G7 | | | |

Verse 1

    G7
I got something to say that might cause you pain.

If I catch you talking to that boy again,

    C7
I'm gonna let you down

    G7
And leave you flat.

    D7♯9
Because I told you before,

C7   **G7**   **D7**
Oh, you can't do that.

Verse 2

           G7
Well, it's the second time I've caught you talking to him.

Do I have to tell you one more time, I think it's a sin?

        C7
I think I'll let you down (Let you down.)

          G7
And leave you flat.

(Gonna let you down and leave you flat.)

         D7$\sharp$9
Because I've told you before,

C7   **G7**
Oh, you can't do that.

Bridge 1

         B7   **Em**
Everybody's green

      Am   **Bm**   **G7**
'Cause I'm the one who won your love.

         B7   **Em**
But if they'd seen

      Am
You talking that way,

      Bm   **D**
They'd laugh in my face.

Verse 3

       G7
So please listen to me if you wanna stay mine,

I can't help my feelings, I'll go out of my mind.

       C7
I'm gonna let you down (Let you down.)

       G7
And leave you flat.

(Gonna let you down and leave you flat.)

       D7♯9
Because I've told you before,

C7   **G7**   **D7**
Oh, you can't do that.

Solo

| **G7** | | | | **C7** | | |
| **G7** | | **D7** | **C7** | **G7** | | |

Bridge 2   *Repeat Bridge 1*

Verse 4

       G7
So please listen to me if you wanna stay mine,

I can't help my feelings, I'll go out of my mind.

       C7
I'm gonna let you down (Let you down.)

       G7
And leave you flat.

(Gonna let you down and leave you flat.)

       D7♯9
Because I've told you before,

C7   **G7**   **D7**
Oh, you can't do that.

You Like Me Too Much

Words and Music by
George Harrison

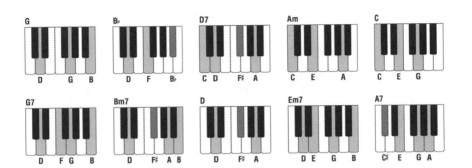

Though you've gone a-way — this morn - ing,

Intro |G |B♭ D7 |G |

Verse 1

       G   Am
Though you've gone away this morning,

           C   G7
You'll be back again to-night

          Am
Telling me there'll be no next time

       C   G7
If I just don't treat you right.

Chorus 1

       Bm7   D7
You'll never leave me and you know it's true,

         G   C   D
'Cause you like me too much and I like you,

Verse 2

        Am
You've tried before to leave me,

        C   **G7**
But you haven't got the nerve

        Am
To walk out and make me lonely,

        C   **G7**
Which is all that I de-serve.

Chorus 2   *Repeat Chorus 1*

Bridge 1

Em7 **A7**
I really do,

        Bm7   **A7**
And it's nice when you be-lieve me.

Em7 A7   **D7**
If   you leave me...

Verse 3

        Am
I will follow you and bring you

C   **G7**
Back where you be-long,

        Am
'Cause I couldn't really stand it.

        C   **G7**
I'd ad-mit that I was wrong.

Chorus 3

        Bm7   **D7**
I wouldn't let you leave me, 'cause it's true,

        G   **C**   **D7**
'Cause you like me too much and I like you,

Solo		G									C				
		G				D7									

```
              G           C              D
'Cause you like me too much and I like you.
```

Bridge 2   *Repeat Bridge 1*

Verse 4
```
        Am
I will follow you

              C                G7
And bring you back where you be-long,

           Am
'Cause I couldn't really stand it.

           C            G7
I'd admit that I was wrong.
```

Chorus 4
```
        Bm7                           D7
I wouldn't let you leave me, 'cause it's true,

              G         C              D
'Cause you like me too much and I like you,

              G         C              D
'Cause you like me too much and I like you.
```

Outro | G | | B♭ D7 | G

You Know My Name
(Look Up the Number)

Words and Music by John Lennon
and Paul McCartney

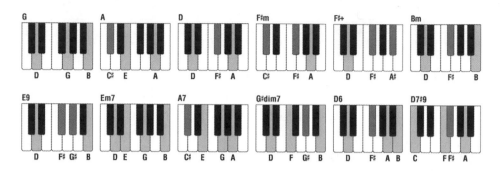

Intro $\left|\text{G/D}\right.$ $\left|\text{A/C}\#\right.$ $\left|\text{D F}\#\text{m}\right|\text{G A}$ $\left|\text{D F}\#\text{m}\right|\text{G A}\left.\right|$

Verse 1

G   F#+ Bm   E9
You know my name,   look up the number.

G   D   Em7   A
You know my name, look up the number.

D F#m   G   A
You, you know, you know my name.

D F#m   G   A   D
You, you know, you know my name.

N.C.
Good evening and welcome to Slaggers,

                   D
Featuring Denis O'Bell

Em7
And Ringo. Hey, Ringo!

D
Let's hear it for Denis!

Em7
(Good evening.)

Verse 2	G F#+ Bm E9

Verse 2

G   F#+ Bm   E9
You know my name,   better look up my number.

G   D   Em7   A
You know my name,   that's right, look up my number.

Verse 3

D   D/F#   G   A
You, you know, you know my name.

D   D/F#   G   A
You, you know, you know my name.

G   F#+   Bm
You know my name, ba, ba, ba, ba, ba, ba, ba, ba, pum,

              E9
Look up my number.

G   D
You know my name.

Em7   A
That's right, look up my number.

Verse 4

      D   **Em7**
Oh, you know, you know,   you know my name.

D   **Em7**
  You know, you know, you know my name.

             G
Huh, huh, huh, huh.

        F♯+   **Bm**
You know my name, ba, ba, ba, pum,

             E9
Look up the number.

G   **D** **Em7**   **A**
You know my name,   look up the number.

D   **Em7**   **A**
You, you know, you know my name, baby.

D   **Em7**   **A**
You, you know, you know my name.

D   **A7**
  You know, you know my name.

D   **A7**
  You know, you know my name.

Oh, let's hear it!

       D **N.C.**
Go on, Den-is, let's hear it for Denis O'Bell.

Verse 5

D   **D/F♯**   **G**   **A**
  You know,   you know,   you know my name.

D   **D/F♯**   **G**   **A**
  You know,   you know,   you know my name.

G N.C.   **F♯+ N.C.**
  You know my name,   look up the number.

Bm N.C.   **E9 N.C.**   **G**
  You know my name,   look up the num-ber.

D   **Em7**   **A**
  You know,   you know my name,   look up the number.

Verse 6

    D   **D/F#**
You know my name,

      G   **A**
You know my number too.

    D   **D/F#**
You know my number three,

      G   **A**
And you know my number four.

D   **D/F#**
 You know my name,

      G   **G#dim7**
You know my number too.

      A
You know my name,

You know my number.

                 D6
What's up with you? Ha!

N.C.
You know my name,

That's right.

Yeah.

Outro |D D/F#|G A |D D/F#|G A |
G	F#+	Bm	E9	G D	Em7	A
D F#m	G A	D F#m	G A
G	F#+	Bm	E9	G D	Em7	A
D F#m	G A	D F#m	G A
D F#m	G G#dim7	A7	D7#9

You Know What to Do

Words and Music by
George Harrison

When I see you, I just___ don't know what to say. ___

| D | A | E | Bm | Bm(maj7) |

Intro | D | | |

Verse 1

         A   E
When I see you, I just don't know what to say.

         A   E
I like to be with you every hour of the day.

Chorus 1

                  A E
So if you want me,

                A E
Just like I need you,

          A   D
You know what to do.

Verse 2

     A   E
I watched you walking by, and you looked all a-lone.

     A   E
I hope that you won't mind if I walk you back home.

Chorus 2

                A E
And if you want me,

                A E
Just like I need you,

          A   D
You know what to do.

Bridge 1

Bm
Just call on me when you are lonely,

Bm(maj7)
I'll keep my love for you only.

A   D
I'll call on you if I'm lonely too.

Verse 3

A   E
Understand, I'll stay with you every day.

A   E
Make you love me more in every way.

Chorus 3

               A E
So if you want me,

                A E
Just like I want you,

         A   D
You know what to do.

Bridge 2

Repeat Bridge 1

Verse 4

Repeat Verse 3

Chorus 4

               A E
So if you want me,

                A E
Just like I want you,

         A   D
You know what to do.

You Never Give Me Your Money

Words and Music by John Lennon
and Paul McCartney

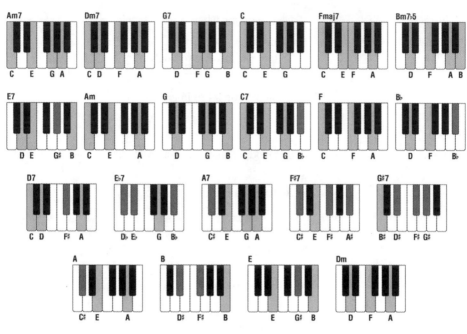

Intro

|Am7 |Dm7 |G7 |C |
|Fmaj7 |Bm7♭5 E7 |Am | |

Verse 1

Am7   Dm7
You never give me your money,

G7   C
You only give me your funny paper.

Fmaj7   Bm7♭5   E7
And in the middle of negot - i - ations

       Am
You break down.

Verse 2

Am7   Dm7
  I never give you my number,

G7   C
  I only give you my situation.

Fmaj7   Bm7♭5   E7
  And in the middle of invest - i - gation

  Am   C/G G
I break down.

Bridge

C   E7
  Out of college, money spent;

Am   C7
See no future, pay no rent.

F   G   C
All the money's gone, nowhere to go.

C   E7
  Any jobber got the sack,

Am   C7
Monday morning turning back,

F   G   C
Yellow lorry slow, nowhere to go.

   B♭   F   C
But oh, that magic feeling, nowhere to go!

B♭   F   C
Oh, that magic feeling, nowhere to go!

Nowhere to go!

| *Interlude* | ‖: B♭ | F | C | :‖ *Play 3 times* |

Ah,   ooh.

| D7 | E♭7 G7 | C7 A7 | E♭7 C7 | F#7 E♭7 | A7 F#7 G7 G#7 |

Verse 3

    A   B
    One sweet dream,

C   E   A
Pick up the bags and get in the limou-sine.

Dm   G/D
Soon we'll be away from here,

Am/D   G/D   A
Step on the gas and wipe that tear away.

                B   C G/B A
One sweet dream   came true   today,

       C G/B A
Came true   today,

       C G/B A
Came true   today,

        C G/B A
Yes it did.

Outro

    C   G/B
‖: One, two, three, four, five, six, seven,

A
All good children go to heaven.   :‖ *Repeat and fade*

You Won't See Me

Words and Music by John Lennon
and Paul McCartney

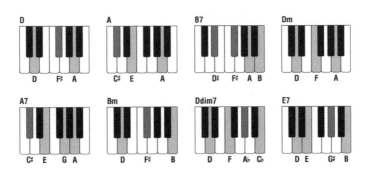

Intro |D   A | |

Verse 1

         A   B7   D   A
When I call you up, your line's en-gaged.

               B7   D   A
I have had e-nough, so act your age.

           A7   D   Dm   A
We have lost the time that was hard to find,

               B7
And I will lose my mind

    D A
If you won't see me,

(You won't see me.)

D A
You won't see me.

Verse 2

                   A   B7   D   A
          I don't know why you should want to hide,

                        B7   D   A
          But I can't get through, my hands are tied.

                    A7   D   Dm   A
          I won't want to stay, I don't have much to say.

                        B7
          But I can turn a-way,

           D   A
          And you won't see me,

          (You won't see me.)

          D   A
          You won't see me.

                   Bm   Dm   Ddim7   A
Bridge 1 Time after time, you re-fuse to even listen.

          B7   D/E   E7
          I wouldn't mind if I knew what I was missing.

                        A   B7   D   A
Verse 3   Though the days are few, they're filled with tears,

                        B7   D   A
          And since I lost you, it feels like years.

                    A7   D   Dm   A
          Yes, it seems so long, girl, since you've been gone,

                        B7
          And I just can't go on.

           D   A
          If you won't see me,

          (You won't see me.)

          D   A
          You won't see me.

Bridge 2   *Repeat Bridge 1*

Verse 4
                         A   B7   D   A
          Though the days are few, they're filled with tears,

                              B7   D   A
          And since I lost you, it feels like years.

                         A7   D   Dm   A
          Yes, it seems so long, girl, since you've been gone,

                              B7
          And I just can't go on.

                          D   A
          If you won't see me,

          (You won't see me.)

          D   A
          You won't see me.

          (You won't see me.)

Outro   ‖: A   │B7   │D   │A   :‖ *Repeat and fade*

You'll Be Mine

By Paul McCartney
and John Lennon

Melody:

When the stars _ fall at night, _

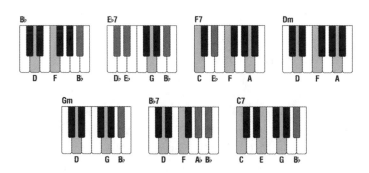

Intro |Bb Eb7 |Bb F7 |

Verse 1

        Bb   Dm   Gm   Bb
When the stars fall at night, you'll be mine, yes I know.

        F7   Eb7
You'll be mine, un-til you die,

        Bb   F7
You'll be mine.

Verse 2

        Bb   Dm Gm   Bb
And so all the night, you'll be mine,   you'll be mine.

        F7   Eb7   Bb
And the stars gonna shine, you'll be mine,

Bb7
Now.

PIANO CHORD SONGBOOK

Bridge

        E♭7
My darling, when you brought me that toast the other morning,

B♭   B♭7
I, I looked into your eyes   and I could see

        E♭7
A National Health eyeball.

             C7
And I loved you like I have never done,

            F7
I have never done be-fore.

Verse 3

        B♭   Dm
Yes, the stars gonna shine

        Gm   B♭
And you'll be mine, and you'll be mine.

        F7   E♭7   B♭
You'll be mine, and the stars gonna shine.

You're Going to Lose That Girl

Words and Music by John Lennon
and Paul McCartney

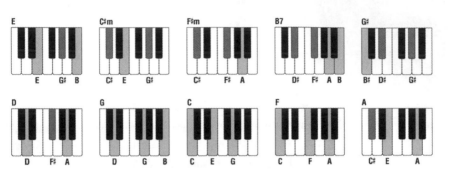

You're gon - na   lose   that   girl. ___

	E **C#m**
Chorus 1	You're gonna lose that girl.
	(Yes, yes, you're gonna lose that girl.)
	F#m **B7**
	You're gonna lose _____ that girl.
	(Yes, yes, you're gonna lose that girl.)

	E **G#**
Verse 1	If you don't take her out tonight,
	F#m **B7**
	She's gonna change her mind.
	(She's gonna change her mind.)
	E **G#**
	And I will take her out tonight,
	F#m **B7**
	And I will treat her kind.
	(I'm gonna treat her kind.)

Chorus 2	*Repeat Chorus 1*

Verse 2

    E   G♯
  If you don't treat her right, my friend,
         F♯m   B7
You're gonna find her gone.
                (You're gonna find her gone.)
  E   G♯
  'Cause I will treat her right and then
         F♯m   B7
You'll be the lonely one.
                (You're not the only one.)

Chorus 3

             E   C♯m
You're gonna lose that girl.
                (Yes, yes, you're gonna lose that girl.)
         F♯m   B7
You're gonna lose _____ that girl.
                (Yes, yes, you're gonna lose that girl.)
         F♯m   D
You're gonna lose. _____ (Yes, yes, you're gonna lose that girl.)

Bridge 1

        G   C   G
  I'll make a point of taking her away from you,

(Watch what you do.) yeah.
                        C   F
The way you treat her, what else can I do?

Solo

‖: E | G♯ | F♯m | B7   :‖

Chorus 4   *Repeat Chorus 3*

Bridge 2   *Repeat Bridge 1*

Verse 3   *Repeat Verse 1*

Chorus 5

             E   C♯m
You're gonna lose that girl.
                (Yes, yes, you're gonna lose that girl.)
         F♯m   B7
You're gonna lose _____ that girl.
                (Yes, yes, you're gonna lose that girl.)
         F♯m   D   A   E
You're gonna lose_____ that girl.

You've Got to Hide Your Love Away

Words and Music by John Lennon
and Paul McCartney

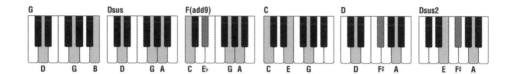

Verse 1

    G   **Dsus** **F(add9) C G**
    Here I stand, head   in hand,

C   **F(add9)** **C**
Turn my face to the wall.

G   **Dsus F(add9) C G**
If she's gone I can't   go on

C   **F(add9)**   **C** **D**
Feeling two foot small.

Verse 2

G **Dsus F(add9) C G**
Ev'rywhere peo - ple stare,

C   **F(add9)** **C**
Each and ev'ry day.

G   **Dsus**   **F(add9) C G**
I can see them laugh   at me,

C   **F(add9)** **C D D/C D/B D/A**
And I hear them say:

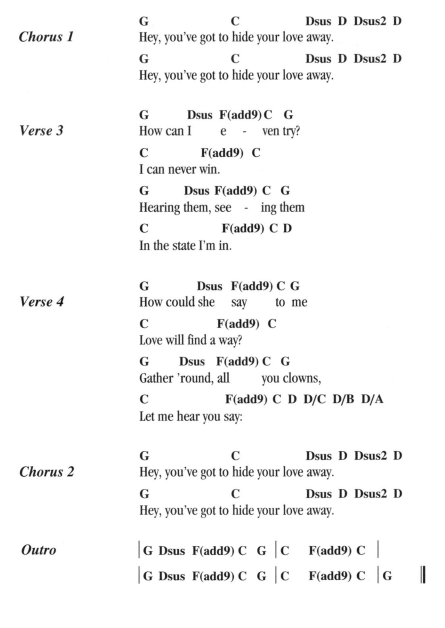

Chorus 1

G   C   Dsus D Dsus2 D
Hey, you've got to hide your love away.

G   C   Dsus D Dsus2 D
Hey, you've got to hide your love away.

Verse 3

G   Dsus F(add9) C G
How can I   e - ven try?

C   F(add9) C
I can never win.

G   Dsus F(add9) C G
Hearing them, see - ing them

C   F(add9) C D
In the state I'm in.

Verse 4

G   Dsus F(add9) C G
How could she   say   to me

C   F(add9) C
Love will find a way?

G   Dsus F(add9) C G
Gather 'round, all   you clowns,

C   F(add9) C D D/C D/B D/A
Let me hear you say:

Chorus 2

G   C   Dsus D Dsus2 D
Hey, you've got to hide your love away.

G   C   Dsus D Dsus2 D
Hey, you've got to hide your love away.

Outro

| G Dsus F(add9) C G | C   F(add9) C |

| G Dsus F(add9) C G | C   F(add9) C | G   ‖

You've Really Got a Hold on Me

Words and Music by
William "Smokey" Robinson

Melody:

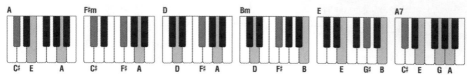

I don't ___ like ___ you, ___

A   F#m   D   Bm   E   A7

C#   E   A   C#   F#   A   D   F#   A   D   F#   B   E   G#   B   C#   E   G   A

Intro |A |F#m |

Verse 1
A
I don't like you, but I love you.

F#m
Seems that I'm always thinking of you.

A   **D**
Oh, oh, oh, you treat me badly,

         Bm
I love you madly.

         E   **A**
You've really got a hold on me. (You've really got a hold on me.)

           F#m
You've really got a hold on me. (You've really got a hold on me.) Baby.

Verse 2
A
I don't want you, but I need you.

F#m
Don't wanna kiss you, but I need to.

A   **D**
Oh, oh, oh, you do me wrong, now.

         Bm
My love is strong,now.

         E   **A**
You've really got a hold on me. (You've really got a hold on me.)

           F#m
You've really got a hold on me. (You've really got a hold on me.) Baby.

	A A7 D

Bridge 1

```
A       A7          D
I love you and all I want you to do is just

A N.C.   A N.C.
Hold me, hold me,

A N.C.   E        N.C.       A
Hold me, hold me.

F♯m  E   A
              Tighter.

F♯m  E   A
              Tighter.
```

Verse 3

```
A
I wanna leave you, don't wanna stay here.

F♯m
Don't wanna spend another day here.

A                   D
Oh, oh, oh, I wanna split now;

          Bm
I just can't quit now.

      E         A
You've really got a hold on me. (You've really got a hold on me.)
                      F♯m
You've really got a hold on me. (You've really got a hold on me.) Baby.
```

Bridge 2

```
A       A7          D
I love you and all I want you to do is just

A N.C.          A N.C.
Hold me, (Please.) hold me, (Squeeze.)

A N.C.   E        N.C.
Hold me, hold me.
```

Outro

```
          A
You've really got a hold on me. (You've really got a hold on me.)
          F♯m                                       A
You've really got a hold on me. (You've really got a hold on me.)
```

Your Mother Should Know

Words and Music by John Lennon
and Paul McCartney

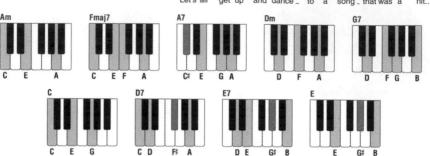

Intro

| Am | | |

Verse 1

Am   **Fmaj7**
Let's all get up and dance to a song

      A7/E   **Dm**
That was a hit before your mother was born.

G7   **C** **C/B** **A7**
Though she was born a long, long time a-go,

        D7
Your mother should know,

G7   **C**
 Your mother should know.

E7
Sing it again.

Verse 2

Am   **Fmaj7**
Let's all get up and dance to a song

     A7/E   **Dm**
That was a hit before your mother was born.

G7   **C** **C/B** **A7**
Though she was born a long, long time a-go,

      D7
Your mother should know,

G7   **C**
 You mother should know.

Interlude 1 |E |Am |Fmaj7| |Fmaj7/G|C |E7 |

Verse 3

```
Am                Fmaj7
Lift up your hearts and sing me a song
          A7/E        Dm
That was a hit before your mother was born.
G7                   C      C/B   A7
Though she was born a long, long time a-go,
                     D7
Your mother should know,
G7                    C
  Your mother should know.
A7                   D7
  Your mother should know,
G7                    C
  Your mother should know.
```

Interlude 2 |E |Am |Fmaj7| |Fmaj7/G|C |

```
E7
Sing it again...
```

Outro

```
Am                Fmaj7
Da, da, da, da, da, da, da, da, da.
          A7/E        Dm
Da, da, da, da, da, da, da, da, da, da, da.
G7                   C      C/B   A7
Though she was born a long, long time a-go,
                     D7        G7
Your mother should know. (Your mother should.)
                     C         A7
Your mother should know, ye - eah.
                     D7        G7
Your mother should know. (Your mother should.)
                     C         A7
Your mother should know, ye - eah.
                     D7        G7
Your mother should know. (Your mother should.)
                     C
Your mother should know, ye - eah.
```